MOOCs

FOCUS SERIES

Series Editor Jean-Charles Pomerol

MOOCs

Design, Use and Business Models

Jean-Charles Pomerol
Yves Epelboin
Claire Thoury

iSTE

WILEY

First published 2015 in Great Britain and the United States by ISTE Ltd and John Wiley & Sons, Inc.

ISTE Ltd
27-37 St George's Road
London SW19 4EU
UK

www.iste.co.uk

John Wiley & Sons, Inc.
111 River Street
Hoboken, NJ 07030
USA

www.wiley.com

Library of Congress Control Number: 2014956807

British Library Cataloguing-in-Publication Data
A CIP record for this book is available from the British Library
ISSN 2051-2481 (Print)
ISSN 2051-249X (Online)
ISBN 978-1-84821-801-7

Contents

Acknowledgements

We, the authors, would like to express our warmest thanks to the staff at the *Université numérique des sciences de la santé et du sport* (UNF3S – Health & Sport Sciences Digital University): Perrine de Coetlogon, Albert-Claude Benhamou, François Kohler, Marcel Spector and the whole team, from whom the leading author of this book learned a great deal whilst he was President of the UNF3S. At UPMC, we have benefited greatly from the helpful and amicable comments made by Pierre Jarraud, Christian Queinnec, Antoine Rauzy and Jean-Marc Labat, all of whom are specialists in distance education. Let us also mention that a French version of this book was published by Éditions Dunod in Paris, entitled: "*Les MOOC, conception, usages et modèles économiques*".

To all those who have directly or indirectly helped us with their comments and feedback, we are very grateful. Nevertheless, we and we alone are responsible for the opinions expressed in this book.

1

What is a MOOC?

1.1. From distance learning to MOOCs

Whilst MOOCs – *Massive Open Online Courses* – undeniably represent a change of scale, they are nevertheless part of the age-old concept of distance learning. Thus, we feel it is relevant to begin this discussion with a brief history of distance learning, in order to highlight the ways in which MOOCs constitute a breakaway, if indeed they are one. This is one of the questions which we examine in this book.

In the United States, distance learning has been a reality since the late 19th Century (see [WAT 91]). Originally, distance learning centers would send students course material and exercises through the postal service; later, audio versions of the classes became available. In 1948, the University of Louisville (Kentucky) signed an agreement with the PBS (Public Broadcasting Service in the US) whereby the university could use the radio as a medium to support distance learning. Between 1950 and 1980, CBS (Columbia Broadcasting System), in collaboration with NYU, broadcast the series "Sunrise Semester", which offered students university credits.

Originally, audio and video cassettes were also sent by post to students wishing to follow such distance-learning courses. At that early stage, one spoke not of "*e-learning*", but of "distance learning". With the televisual revolution, numerous filmed lectures are put only on YouTube and many video servers at universities, but also on iTunes and other servers. A great many institutions also offer online courses; an example is MIT, with its free program *OpenCourseWare*, launched in 2001. Thereafter, a variety of other, increasingly-sophisticated online learning initiatives have been launched, including *Stanford Engineering Everywhere* (SEE), set up by Andrew Ng in 2007, offering a full course with university credits earned, or the *Open Learning Initiative* (OLI) offered by Carnegie Mellon University. In France, a television channel, Canal U, broadcasts numerous courses offered by prestigious institutions such as the Sorbonne or the *Collège de France*.

In addition, although it is not entirely in the domain of higher education, it is also worth mentioning the Khan Academy which, since 2006, has been making short educational videos publicly available, with a growing degree of success.

Between filmed versions of ordinary classes and courses enriched with videos or documents, there is one constant: the class is delivered to a listener or viewer upon whom no demand at all is made. Strictly speaking, he or she need only switch on the radio/television/computer. In this scenario, *the student is a passive receiver; there is no exchange between the teacher and the student*. In Quebec, thanks to the actions of certain pioneers such as the high-level politician Gilbert Paquette, the tele-university TELUQ (www.teluq.ca/), set up in 1972, very quickly made a name for itself as a major player in distance higher education. Today, it caters to around 18,000 students each year, taking 400 courses. In Quebec, the tele-university is simply a university like any other. It was briefly attached to the University of Quebec, but then regained its independence.

The *Open University* in Great Britain is, indubitably, the most accomplished example of *e-learning* as it was conceived before the dawn of the Internet. In addition to the elements described above, the "OU" makes widespread use of television, and offers full-fledged university-level courses, run in parallel to those delivered on site at universities and equivalent to those courses in status.

From the end of the 1990s onwards, we see the development of the Internet. At the start, this enabled universities to distribute Word and

PDF versions of paper brochures, and later audio files and finally, video files as well. In addition, the dawn of the Internet enabled students to register online, meaning it became possible for the content providers to monitor the amount of audience their classes were receiving. To begin with, there was no interaction with the teacher: it was a "*one-way*", or "*top-down*", approach.

Gradually, following the advent of *Web 2.0*, a very significant degree of interaction became possible. Forums were set up where students could make comments, engage in "*chats*" to interact with other students and with their teachers, and complete exercises online. In order to access these classes, it was necessary to register – i.e. the system could only be used by registered students and staff, as is the case in conventional universities. Certain universities then began to specialize in this type of distance learning. These were termed *open universities* – a nod to the British *Open University* set up in 1969. The *Open University*, which already had a significant body of experience acquired before the Web was born, now serves 100,000 registered students, and confers degrees on its students, who are clearly identified. The *Open University* is a true university, whose students live all over the country.

Western Governors University (WGU) – an entirely virtual university, set up in 1997, on the initiative of 19 US State Governors – also provides a very good example of the use of new technologies in higher education, before the dawn of MOOCs. Today WGU educates 45,000 students online for a tution of $3,000 per six-month term.

Additionally, at each university at local level, students have an Internet account, and what is known as a Digital Work Environment (DWE). Using this account, they can access files, and therefore classes, exercises, photos and videos, and interact with their teachers. Obviously, these accounts are personal, and strictly reserved for registered students. These environments are managed by the universities. Provided they have sufficient bandwidth, students can follow a filmed class, either in real time or time-shifted, from their homes (which relieves the issue of overcrowding in lecture theaters) and, once it has been recorded, the class remains accessible; students may watch it and re-watch it as many times as they wish. This is the system adopted by many universities in France – particularly the Faculty of Medicine at UPMC, which has employed this system since 2007, for first-year teaching of medicine. It is also possible to distribute the material on CD-ROM; that solution was adopted by the University of Grenoble in 2006, for its first-year medicine teaching, under the guidance of a specialist in digital education, Daniel Pagonis and Jean-Paul Romanet, the Dean of the university, before the system was made entirely available online. At the NYU School of Medicine, and at the *Université Lyon*, 3D anatomy courses have been being made available online for many years. Many of these pioneering organizations also put exercises online. This is common practice in the teaching of computer science at UPMC, and in many other universities as well, because in computer science, it is possible to set a programming exercise and monitor its solution remotely.

In relation to these experiments, it cannot be said that MOOCs mark a new departure in terms of content. It is in the relationship between the teachers and the learners that the "revolution" lies, if indeed there is a revolution. To use the typical language of pedagogy, it can now be said that the learner is "at the heart of the system", in the sense that he or she is no longer supposed to be a passive "receiver", but rather an essential active player in his or her own learning. We hear the echo of the old adage employed by the teachers of yesteryear: to learn, you have to *want* to learn! Now, though, it is becoming possible and visible, because signing up for a MOOC is a deliberate commitment on the part of the learner, and so, as we shall see later on, is following that course to the very end.

The following diagram, taken from Wikipedia, illustrates the trajectory which, in the United States, led to the development of the concept of a MOOC, from its beginnings in online courses, on the one hand, and open universities on the other. Distance learning has never ceased to evolve since the birth of the open universities, the *OpenCourseWare* program piloted at MIT, followed by Harvard, and it has now birthed the concept of a MOOC as we know it today. Looking at the continuum shown in Figure 1.1, we can clearly see, firstly, that there is no significant change of direction and, secondly, if we overlook the possible pedagogical implications, we can state that *MOOCs are distance learning as the order of the day.* We shall see that this affirmation is not false, but that it is, nevertheless, rather simplistic!

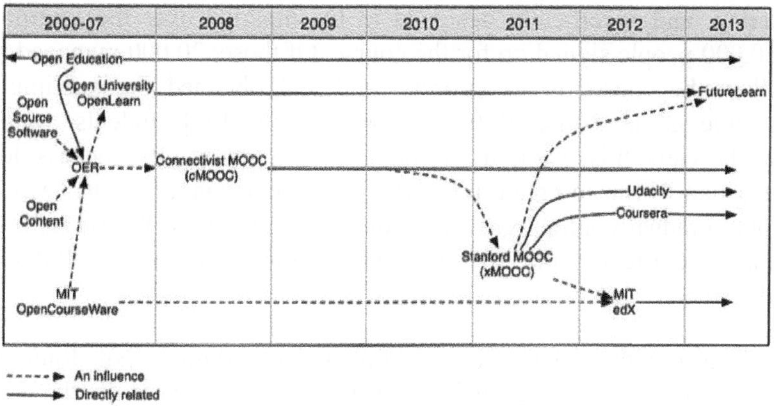

Figure 1.1. *History of MOOCs. Figure drawn from Wikipedia*

One of the changes in relation to this restrictive vision is the relationship between the teacher and the student, and the place of face-to-face teaching in these programs. Later on, we shall look again in greater detail at the importance of this accompaniment of distance learning by a presence-based program more or less "driven" by the questions raised by the students. This could be called "*reverse learning*", because in this scenario it is the student who asks the questions and thereby, to a certain extent, "directs" his or her own learning.

1.2. What is a MOOC?

The phenomenon of MOOCs, and the term itself, arose in the United States. The birth of the first MOOC can be pinpointed to 2008 [COR 10]: the launch of an interactive online training course, by George Siemens and Stephen Downes, on "*Connectivism and Connective Knowledge*"[1]. This course attracted several thousand participants all over the world. However, the first MOOC which truly

1 See https//sites.google.com/site/themoocguide/3-cck08–the-distributed-course.

catered to enormous numbers of subscribers was launched in the fall of 2011 by Professor Sebastian Thrun from Stanford. Thrun placed online a course on artificial intelligence, taught by himself and Peter Norvig, and specifically designed to be imparted over the Internet: 160,000 people signed up for the course. Of those, 20,000 managed to follow the course in its entirety, and 364 obtained the maximum possible grade. None of those 364 were Stanford students. Many people view this event as a major turning point. Its success led Sebastian Thrun to create his own start-up company, *Udacity*, which would gradually attract growing numbers of investors. Within its first year of existence, the site gained a following of nearly 400,000 subscribers.

Two months later, Daphne Koller and Andrew Ng founded *Coursera* – one of the first and best-known platforms in the US. *Coursera* now has more than 10 million students in 190 countries, and offers nearly 600 online courses; as compared with 2 million students and 200 courses for *edX* and fewer than 100 courses for *Udacity*. The site www.mooc-list.com offers an up-to-date list of all existing MOOCs.

MOOCs are defined by their audience and their format. These courses are open to one and all, and have no physical limitations because they are completely digitized and accessible over the Internet with no barriers. They may or may not be free, are accessible from any computer or tablet, and facilitate mass diffusion of knowledge. Yet as has been stated already, *students must register in order to follow the courses*, unlike with filmed classes shown on television. A MOOC is a tool which, to a certain extent, can be personalized by whoever is using it. Many MOOCs are cadenced; the pace at which the student is able to follow the course becomes an element for assessment. This means that there is a starting session, new material introduced during the session, exercises for students to do each week, quizzes and evaluations. Maintaining the pace and completing the exercises is a crucial element for gaining the certification. There are two ways in which to pursue this course: all at the same time, in a set session (thus there is a timetable for everybody), or indeed individually at a chosen time (with everyone being free to follow it whenever he or she is able to or wishes to). As it is easier to remotely monitor who has done the exercises than it is to evaluate the quality of their answers, MOOCs are sometimes assessed more on the basis of the participation and assiduousness than the competence of the subscriber, with the person's competence being evaluated separately by way of the answers to the quizzes and exercises.

MOOCs are said to be "*massive*" because, as there are no prerequisites, the number of subscribers may, potentially, be very great. Thus, it is by the "massive" number of those subscribers that the MOOC is characterized, although it is still necessary to distinguish those who sign up from those who actually follow the course right through to the end. Certain MOOCs are followed by tens or hundreds of thousands of people, but this is not true of all such courses. The course is said to be massive as soon as it gains a sufficiently high number of subscribers – a much higher number than could possibly be envisaged with face-to-face teaching, ranging from a few hundred to over 150,000 students for the best-known MOOCs. Note, though, that this does not mean that all the subscribers actually follow the course. We shall come back to this point later on. We have already mentioned the 160,000 students registered on the MOOC in Artificial Intelligence offered by Stanford. The MOOC run by Martin Odersky at EPFL (*Ecole Polytechnique Fédérale de Lausanne*) on the SCALA programming language has catered for 50,000 people since it went online. This question of the number of people enrolled on the course – is it a characteristic of MOOCs or of *e-learning*? In other words, if a MOOC is taken by only twenty people, is it still a MOOC? The question is somewhat controversial, and "MOOCers" cannot find agreement on the subject. It becomes something of a philosophical issue, which inevitably evokes the story of the Ship of Theseus, all of whose parts have gradually been replaced: can it still be said to be the same ship? However, the question seems to be becoming less and less theoretical because, as we shall see, MOOCs for small groups certainly have a promising future. It should also be noted that, as the EPFL's experience testifies, a MOOC taught in English attracts ten times more people than a MOOC taught in French. The same is true for other languages.

MOOCs are also "*open*", which refers to the fact that enrolment is unrestricted, open to all audiences, and is not conditioned by enrolment at the particular university or attainment of a particular level of study or professional status. However, the "*open*" in MOOC does not mean *Open Source* or *Open Access*; in other words, the software and the content are not necessarily open. Thus, it is not necessarily possible to retrieve the content in order to modify it, or the data of the participants. Neither does the word "*open*" signify "free".

A MOOC is "*online*", meaning that all the courses and exercises are organized for delivery on the Internet. It is not just a question of putting the content of the classes online, otherwise we would speak of "content distribution". In a MOOC, there is a true pedagogical agenda, a progression. Exercises, homework and sometimes even exams are online. It is possible to follow the course from absolutely anywhere, provided one has access to the Web – not only on the benches in the university. Finally, a MOOC can be personalized and adapted to the pace desired by the student.

MOOCs are massive and open: the teaching is available not only to ten-odd students in a particular establishment, but to students all over the world. However, it should be noted that a MOOC, although it is open, registers its students; the organizers know who the students are; however, registration is free and there are no prerequisites. The fact that the courses are open to the general public means that when somebody asks a question on the forum attached to the course, they address not only the teachers but all the other taking the course at the same time, the world over. This gives rise to a new degree of autonomy, because the student does not only interact with the teacher; the students interact with one another; they can offer one another help, suggestions about modules to come, exercises to be done, etc.; they "construct" their course with their fellows. Here, we enter into the logic of collective knowledge construction; it is no longer a simple transmission of information or knowledge.

For example, Shimon Shocken, who gave a MOOC on computer science, posted a problem online with all the elements needed to solve it. That same evening, he realized that a student had asked a question on the forum, and at the same time as he, the teacher, was writing an answer, he noticed that there was already a very large number of responses. Reading over the various messages posted on the forum, he realized that the Internet users, between them, had constructed the correct answer, and thus constructed the whole piece of knowledge. This phenomenon gives rise to emulation between the students following the MOOC.

Certain people speak of "*flipped teaching*" or "*flipped classrooms*" because, whilst it is important to avoid naively adopting the idealistic view of the student teaching the teacher, the exclusive link from the teacher to the student is called into question[2]. Let us state that now, firstly, the interactions take place in both directions, and secondly, they occur between all the learners. It is in this regard that MOOCs truly differ from conventional online teaching or filmed classes. In light of a minimal definition put forward by a pioneer in the teaching of computer science online, Christian Queinnec, it can be said that *a MOOC is distance learning, accompanied by assessment which is also, essentially, remote, associated with social networks which favor exchanges between students*.

The co-founder of *Coursera*, Daphne Koller, states that she wishes to transform the passive time of students who, in class, listens to the educator transmit his/her expertise, into active time. This vision is a summary of the concept of flipped teaching: "*lectures at home and homework in class*". If the lesson is available online, on the Web, the students can watch it before and/or after class. In this case, the class can become a time for exchanges which, instead of transmission from the teacher to the students (vertically), take place between the students (horizontally) and, ultimately, from the students to the teacher as well. The learner is engaged in an active learning approach. As Marcel Lebrun says on his blog (http://lebrunremy.be/WordPress/): "*the less I teach, the more they learn*"[3]. What must be understood is that what happens after class is more important than the class itself. According to the proponents of *Coursera*, the role of the teacher is destined to

2 The term "*flipped learning*" dates from 2007, originally introduced by two secondary-school teachers – Jonathan Bergmann and Aaron Sams – who posted their classes on YouTube so their students could prepare for them at home.

3 Original French: *moins j'enseigne, plus ils apprennent.*

change considerably over the years; from their point of view, the interaction is founded primarily on the fact of finding the correct response. In addition, the popularization of the Internet now enables everyone to have access to information, and to raw knowledge, thanks – amongst other things – to encyclopedias such as Wikipedia. Consequently, the teacher no longer has a monopoly on the transmission of knowledge and – which is more – the student can become aware of the limits of the teacher's own knowledge. In addition, we notice an increasing number of students who, even during the class, run searches to verify what the teacher is saying. In France, lecture theaters, for first-year students, have become spaces where, more often than not, students check on their tablets and, with their peers comment on the teacher's discourse. This may prove extremely challenging for teachers who have the feeling that their students are no longer truly listening. It is important to replace lecture-theater classes with MOOCs – a point to which we shall come back later. With MOOCs, the learners have the opportunity to interact, and the teachers are capable of adapting to the expectations and the levels of the students, which MOOCs help to pinpoint much more easily than correcting a homework assignment from time to time.

1.3. xMOOCs, cMOOCs and other SPOCs

Beyond the characteristics which are common to all types of MOOCs, we can distinguish two main types: one which we shall call "classic", which entails the design of a MOOC which, like a teacher, guides the students following it, along a clearly-defined path; this is an "xMOOC" or "transmissive MOOC". The other type, called a "connectivist" MOOC, is much less directive. The material is made available to the learners, but it is the learners themselves who construct their own course, manage their progression and, by interaction with other learners, construct their own learning. This is known as a cMOOC[4].

4 See the discussion given by J. Mackness about the differences between cMOOCs and xMOOCs: http://jennymackness.wordpress.com/2013/10/22/cmoocs-and-xmoocs-key-differences/.

1.3.1. *xMOOCs*

An xMOOC is fairly close to the classic pedagogical model, because first and foremost, it is an existing course, made available online. According to Stephen Downes, the "x" denotes the presence of an eXtension to conventional teaching, in the same vein as MITx, which is the extension to MIT's campus[5]. This course is supplemented by directed tasks, practical work, orientation toward online documentation, and evaluations. The knowledge is found on the MOOC, it is declared, and the course is, in principle, coherent and progressive. The learning objective and the nature of the acquisitions are predefined by the designer of the MOOC.

The primary objective of an xMOOC is the transmission of knowledge. Given its proximity to the conventional model of a course, an xMOOC requires a not-insignificant amount of individual activity, in spite of the existence of forums and peer correction, which is sometimes envisaged. Platforms such as *Coursera* or *edX* essentially offer xMOOCs.

Consider, for example, the xMOOCs offered by EPFL. These MOOCs are led by teaching staff. Certain MOOCs are aimed at improving the internal service provision in order to facilitate better teaching, using the flipped-classrooms model, with greater contact between the students and teachers and the deliberate absence of lecture-theater classes during the first year. There are also MOOCs with high visibility on the world stage, which are designed to promote the reputation of EPFL, by attracting participants from all over the world. Initial feedback from EPFL suggests that it is not certain that the school will do away with face-to-face lectures; they are not yet sure whether they wish to pursue the model to its full extent. For now, students have the choice between taking a conventional course and taking the MOOC.

The introductory MOOC on cell networks offered by Telecom Bretagne (Jean-Marie Gilliot) affords us another example. The description of the course is very precise, the objectives are declared and,

5 https://plus.google.com/+StephenDownes/posts/LEwaKxL2MaM.

although the knowledge required and the intended audience are not clearly defined, the format of the MOOC is rigidly structured. At the heart of it, this type of MOOC is similar to open *e-learning*. In the view of Matthieu Cisel[6], the difference lies in the multiplicity of the activities set in addition to the classes. These activities may be for individual or group work, and the evaluations can be corrected either by the students themselves or by their peers. Generally, an xMOOC comprises 6 to 12 sessions; each sequence lasts around ten minutes, on top of which comes the time taken for exercises and the various activities. A session typically involves 1 hour of video, 3-4 hours of personal time to complete the exercises, and the time taken for reading.

1.3.2. *cMOOCs*

A cMOOC is a so-called *connectivist* MOOC (hence the "c"). It is based on a participative approach whereby each student carries out his or her own search for the best way forward, conducts exchanges with his or her peers and publishes his or her own conclusions. The pedagogical model is innovative, the knowledge is distributed, and partly self-generated, and the coherence of the course and the progression is constructed by the learner. The participants can enrich the MOOC, and the community helps to construct and distribute the content. A cMOOC is similar to the vision of free software, with a very prevalent sense of community. It falls into the category of a participative approach[7].

A cMOOC favors an open teaching style, and is based on networks of content and of individuals. According to Wikipedia,

6 Matthieu Cisel is a doctoral candidate at the ENS, Cachan, who has taken a passionate interest in the "MOOC Revolution". Readers can consult his blog at http://blog.educpros.fr/matthieu-cisel/2013/06/30/une-typologie-des-mooc/.

7 In his blog, Matthieu Cisel extends the idea of co-construction to research, whereby communities contribute to the construction of knowledge, with the slogan: "Osez la MOOR" (*Massive On-Line Open Research*). (In its original form, this makes a pun, as it sounds identical to an age-old French piece of wisdom: "*Osez l'amour*" – dare to love. A similar pun can be made in translation if we render the phrase as "Dare to do MOOR". See: http://blog.educpros.fr/matthieu-cisel/2013/09/20/osez-la-moor/.

"connectivism" is a concept developed by George Siemens and Stephen Downes, wishing to revisit the question of learning in the digital age in a networked world. One of the seminal works in this area is "*A learning theory for the digital age*", written by Siemens in 2004[8]. The fundamental notion is that of a network. The first ever connectivist MOOC – strictly speaking, the first MOOC, period – was that run by George Siemens and Stephen Downes, launched in 2008, relating, precisely, to connectivism! In a cMOOC, the teacher's job is not to transmit knowledge to the students, but rather to facilitate exchanges between the participants about a topic.

There are many known examples of connectivist MOOCs. For instance, the aim of the MOOC *Itypa*[9] (*Internet Tout y est Pour Apprendre* – The Internet: All you Need to Learn) is to enable the participants to learn from the possibilities offered by the Net. It is directly inspired by Siemens and Downes' original MOOC. With *Itypa*, there is no formal evaluation carried out, and no diploma or certificate is awarded on completion. Each participant is completely independent, and nobody is duty-bound to hand in any produced work.

The MOOC offered by the University of Edinburgh, entitled "*E-learning and Digital Culture*" also falls into this category. In order to obtain the certification, the participants have to create a digital object, which is evaluated by their peers.

Stephen Downes[10] explains his vision of a MOOC thus. Each student has to choose the content which is most appropriate for his or her needs and objectives. The MOOC is distributed: each participant can use the software to make their own contributions. Downes stresses the fact that a MOOC must encourage participation and contribution from those following it; there is no one piece of knowledge which serves everybody; the goal is interaction and exchange, facilitating the production of additional elements of knowledge.

8 See www.ingedewaard.net/papers/connectivism/2005-siemens-ALearningTheoryfortheDigitalAge.pdf

9 http://itypa.mooc.fr/.

10 http://tipes.wordpress.com/2012/07/18/les-cours-en-ligne-ouverts-et-massifs-explication-en-francais-par-stephen-downes/.

The table below is revised on the basis of that produced by Jean-Marie Gilliot, from Telecom Bretagne, who designed France's first ever MOOC. The model is taken from his personal Website, which contains suggestions of innovative techniques for use in higher education[11]. This table very clearly draws the distinction between a connectionist MOOC (an xMOOC), which is similar to a traditional course, and a connectivist MOOC (a cMOOC), which is designed to be far more innovative.

	Based on traditional courses	Based on the connectivist model
Pedagogical model	Conventional: Lectures – Applied work – Practicals – Evaluations	Connectivism
Knowledge	In class – declared	Distributed – generated
Coherence	Given by the teacher	Constructed by the learner
Learning objectives	Defined by the teacher	Defined by each individual participant for his/her own purposes
Learning	Following the pre-set course	Navigating, forging connections
Resources	Defined in class	Contributed by the participants, in abundance
Exchanges with peers	Possible	Extremely important
Interactions	Forums on Website	Distributed; starting from a shared portal, each participant constructs their own blog
Synchronization	Pace set by the course designer	As and when convenient for participants
Resonance		Between peers
Encouraging independence and self-regulation		Mastery of e-skills

11 http://tipes.wordpress.com/2012/06/12/differents-types-de-moocs/.

Innovation- and impact-oriented	Discipline-oriented	Interdisciplinary by nature
	Based on traditional courses	Based on the connectivist model
Certification	Attached to a university or to particular companies	Attached to a university or peer assessment (badges)[12]
Continuous assessment	Automated	Between peers
Technical platform	Centralized	Web: Virtual Learning Environment
Position of the teacher	Professor depositing knowledge in students	Facilitator

Table 1.1. *The different types of MOOC*

According to *Unow* and Matthieu Cisel[13], there are five criteria which distinguish an xMOOC from a cMOOC: the objective of the course, the level of prerequisites to enroll, the type of resources used, the type of activities offered and the degree of constraint.

An xMOOC is an academic MOOC, which means that it is necessarily attached to an assessment system appropriate for the academic objectives; the goal of an xMOOC (which is far more traditional than that of a cMOOC) is to transmit knowledge. With a cMOOC, on the other hand, the goal is rather the co-construction of content, the objectives are not set in stone, and each participant can make use of the tool as he or she sees fit.

Certain MOOCs claim to be both connectionist and connectivist. For example, we could cite the MOOC *Courlis*[14], run by François Kohler at the University of Lorraine, on the subject of Applied Statistics. Here, the “xMOOC” part is led by the course teachers, and

12 “Badges” are a form of electronic certification which has only recently been introduced. For further information, see: https://backpack.openbadges.org/share/55751ea38a1c3cd8ee5e1d7298e919fd/.

13 http://blog.educpros.fr/matthieu-cisel/2013/06/25/mooc-une-proposition-de-grille-de-lecture/.

14 https://courlis-pf.univ-lorraine.fr.

relates to the selection of resources, as the objective is to create as few resources as possible. A particular piece of work is set each week, with participants expected to bring additional knowledge to the table from outside the course. Some of the exercises are corrected by the students themselves and some by their peers. The cMOOC part of the course enables students to give exercises and examples of the application of the topic in their own domains of expertise. This part of the MOOC is much freer, much less rigid, but is fairly limited.

Finally, there are more possible prefixes than "x" or "c" for MOOCs. Jean-Marie Gilliot employs the term "iMOOC" for *investigation*-based learning, and examples can be found of "tMOOCs" for *task*-oriented MOOCs, or "pMOOCs" for *project*-based MOOCs.

1.3.3. *SPOCs*

Ultimately, in the characterization of MOOCs, we have just seen that the "massive" aspect, referring to a very large number of registered students, is not a very clear concept. Indeed, once a course is put online, the potential audience opened up is absolutely immense. However, does the number of people who actually sign up for the course change the nature of the object? Absolutely not. Hence, we can conceive of MOOCs designed for a limited audience: specifically, the students enrolled on a conventional program at a university. To speak of an online class specifically designed for an audience of students enrolled on a particular course, imparted by the teaching team, we have recently seen the emergence of the term "SPOC: *small private online courses*". This term was popularized by Armando Fox, head of online education at Berkeley, who has become a zealous proponent of SPOCs after having experienced online teaching himself, on a "software engineering" course taught with David Patterson [FOX 13]. The acronym "TORC" is sometimes heard as well: it means "*tiny online restricted courses*".

At the heart of it, a SPOC is a MOOC designed for a class of students who are registered at a university in the conventional manner. We shall see later on that a SPOC is a tool for changing the pedagogical perspective. With a SPOC, the teachers' hope is that the students will become active participants in their own learning formation: "*...if MOOCs are used as a supplement to classroom teaching rather than being viewed a replacement for it, they can increase instructor leverage, student throughput, student mastery, and student engagement. I call this model the SPOC...*" [FOX 13]. Hence, if MOOCs are destined, if not to revolutionize then at least to change teaching in universities, this should result in an explosion in the number of SPOCs. We shall come back to the topic of MOOCs and pedagogy in Chapter 5.

1.3.4. *SOOCs*

One of the difficulties encountered with MOOCs is the diversity of the levels of the students, and the lack of any prerequisites which could account, in part, for the failure rate. We shall revisit this point later on. Hence, there has been a recent development: Small Open Online Courses (SOOCs) are now running, where all students wishing to take the course are obliged to take a test beforehand to determine their level. Amar Kumar[15], from Pearsons Labs, views MOOCs as a sort of Russian nesting doll, with the three levels of courses offered on the basis of the same documentation: MOOCs, SOOCs and SPOCs.

15 "Will SOOCs eat MOOCs for breakfast?", A. Kumar, Pearsons labs, http://labs.pearson.com/will-soocs-eat-moocs-for-breakfast/.

2

How to Construct a MOOC

2.1. From a conventional course to a MOOC

In a conventional course, the teacher stands alone in front of their students. The preparation and writing of the course, therefore, are essentially solitary tasks. The same is true even for large-scale teaching units, where there are parallel classes for directed work: the teaching team gives exercises and their corrections to everyone. A certain part of the preparative work may be done collectively, but ultimately, the teacher alone is in control of what they deliver to the students.

In its initial conception, a MOOC is not greatly different from a traditional course. The main difference lies in the supporting personnel who are needed to implement a MOOC:

– contributions must be filmed, edited and posted online. This requires the support of qualified technicians;

– the course needs to be accompanied by written and illustrated documents. In conventional education, not all professors hand out notes in class. They may choose to refer to books which are available in the university library. For a MOOC, the content needs to be provided in its entirety – either written by the teachers or freely available on the Web (OER, *Open Educational Resources*). The task of composing support materials goes far beyond the compilation of a simple reading list;

– usually, it is necessary to provide online exercises, in the form of quizzes. This requires additional thought, in relation to both the content and the form, as a quiz does not have the same degree of flexibility as does a conventional exercise on paper, corrected by human beings.

All MOOC designers also emphasize the technical quality of the documentation they use – be it in video or written format. This is similar to the requirements when writing a book. A set of notes is essentially judged on the basis of its content, and far less on its form and the quality of the diagrams and illustrations. For a MOOC, quite differently, it is necessary to completely review the formatting, and most of the time, this can only be done by specialists. Few teachers have the knowledge and talent that are so crucial to do this. Fewer still are actually prepared to invest the time needed.

With regard to the illustrations, the problem of copyright must not be forgotten: although it is permissible to reproduce figures and illustrations found in the literature, for a set of notes or a private document, citing the source, it is forbidden for a MOOC which, by definition, is open to the entire world. Short textual quotes may be used, with a clear indication of authorship, but for any graphs, images or other illustrations, it is imperative to obtain permission from the rights holders. Finding those rights holders and obtaining authorization from them is a full-time job in itself, and in practically impossible; it is therefore quicker and more effective to simply redraw the illustrations, but it is not possible to do that for photos. This issue is most problematic for an academic course, and can even become an obstacle to the development of certain photograph-based MOOCs – e.g. in geography or geology.

One final point: most MOOCs, or at least xMOOCs, are organized with a set rhythm, week by week. This is a very important point for the pedagogical approach; an experiment attempted in San José[1] reveals that the lack of an agenda is catastrophic, with most students obtaining a poor score, and the main reason for this seems to be the

1 http://techcrunch.com/20/3/07/19/san-jose-states-bold-experiment-in-on-line-ed-disappoints-suspends-pilot-with-udacity/.

degree of freedom allowed to the students in terms of the pace of their studies. This is very new to most teachers, because in certain countries, it is rare to provide a course plan, at the start of the semester, with a strict agenda of progression. The teachers evaluate the progress, approximately (at least the first time) and empirically adapt the agenda over the course of the semester, depending on the students' responses. In a MOOC, this tempo must be set in advance, and the workload required each week needs to be correctly evaluated; otherwise there is a risk of discouraging the most motivated participants and increasing a dropout rate which is already extremely high. The course needs to be "storyboarded", meaning that, as happens with the production of a movie or a cartoon, each sequence is more or less "self-contained", but the progression from one to the next is carefully calculated to sustain the desire to move on to the next sequence. This is very important: the density of the sequences in a MOOC is very different to that of a face-to-face course; in a MOOC the sequences must be short (see below).

Thus, a MOOC is a project which requires the bringing together of very diverse skill sets. Like any team project, it needs to be coordinated and supervised; put briefly, it requires a project manager to run it. As one may imagine, most teachers are unlikely to be willing to add this to the existing workload from their primary position. They do not all possess the necessary skill.

2.2. Human resources for the building of a MOOC

2.2.1. *Teaching staff*

Teachers are the project commissioners: they define the objectives of the course and how it is to progress. They also work together with the project manager, drafting textual content and appearing in videos.

Quite unlike with a conventional course, where there is no obligation for teachers to provide written notes, they have to write all of the textual elements, supplemented with links to documents available on the Web. More important is the need to appear in videos. Not everybody is equally gifted in public speaking. Some may be at ease in a classroom in front of a small audience, but not in front of a camera. Mediocre, shy or hesitant orators, whom we all know and who are accepted because they have other qualities, would prove absolutely catastrophic in the videos made for MOOCs. Let us state it plainly: it is almost necessary to hold auditions, as happens with cinema, to find the right actors for each role.

This point is interesting, because one of the arguments advanced by the earliest designers of MOOCs and the main consortiums is the possibility they afford to ordinary people to study with the very best teachers – i.e. to their minds, with the most renowned researchers in their fields. However, the best researchers may not necessarily be the best orators – particularly in front of a camera. Some may even refuse to appear on camera.

The teachers being filmed also need to be chosen on the basis of their "screen presence", which is not a common attribute in the university community.

2.2.2. *Instructional designer*

An instructional designer is a hybrid role, lying in the intermediary zone between teaching and digital engineering. This person needs to be conversant with the capabilities of the device which is to be used, and therefore have a good knowledge of the LMS (Learning Management System), whilst at the same time having teaching skills, so as to be able to make suggestions and guide the teacher, who is solely responsible for the content. The designer helps the teacher to storyboard the course, construct the detailed week-to-week plan, and link together the sequences of activities: videos, documents to read, homework (which may or may not need to be handed in) and questionnaires to fill in. At once, he or she assists in the project management and participates in the project oversight. It is desirable that their education enable them to grasp the content of the course in order to better appreciate the issues at hand, and adequately evaluate the tempos and rhythms which need to be put in place. In science, for example, it would be beneficial for the designer to have taken a science-based qualification, supplemented by aspects specific to the professions of digital engineering and teaching.

An alternative is to employ monitors – e.g. doctoral candidates – to deal with the science-related aspects, and have them work in close collaboration with a designer specializing in digital teaching and in the platform used, even if their own background is different.

2.2.3. *Video*

The quality of the course videos, in sequences of 10 to 15 minutes maximum, is an essential point in the evaluation of a MOOC. This may seem like rather a short time. In fact, though, it has been shown that the degree of attention paid when watching a video decreases fairly rapidly. Philip Guo[2] has shown that human attention span decreases very greatly beyond 9-12 minutes. Thus, the course sequences need to be divided up so as to conform to the format of the videos which the students are used to watching on YouTube!

The task of production of the video is divided into two stages: the recording of the professor's discourse and the editing. The teacher needs to have the patience necessary to perform multiple (sometimes many) "takes", because any hesitations or stammers which would barely even be noticed in a lecture theater are disastrous for the quality of a recording. In situation, it is best for the teacher to work in front of an interactive whiteboard or with a graphic tablet, which they use to illustrate what is being said, by writing additional material and supplementing the images projected on screen. Being filmed whilst simply sitting still and reading a text will do nothing at all to help the students maintain attention.

This requires the use of an equipped studio – preferably with several cameras, as it is best to be able to switch between different angles of view. Secondly, the video technician edits the film, choosing the best sequences if several takes have been recorded, and editing out any silences or stumbles. It may take up to four hours to record a one-hour lecture, because of the need for repeated takes and inevitable dead times. The smooth editing of that hour requires a minimum of

2 Philip Guo, "Optimal Video Length for Student Engagement", https://www.edx.org/blog/optimal-video-length-student-engagement/.

thirty hours. That length of time could be reduced, but to the detriment of the quality, and the quality of the videos is the most important judgment criterion used by the participants in a MOOC.

It is not easy to follow a videoed course. Thus, the filmmakers need to work on alternating views and on the quality of the video in order to help the learners maintain attention. This is one of the most critical points for the running of a MOOC, because the equipment and the staff need to be available for the necessary length of time. Numerous universities employ motivated students who are already experts in video matters to surmount this difficulty.

In order to acquire or develop capacities to create videos, it is preferable, where possible, to use "multimedia teams" or "new information technologies teams" which are already present in many major universities.

From the examples given above, we can see that there is no solution of continuity between putting a lecture online, managing interaction with the students, creating videos and finally running a MOOC. For this reason, when constructing a team to build a MOOC, it is best to already have an experienced multimedia team: indeed, in our view, it is absolutely essential.

2.2.4. *Graphic designers and webmasters*

As mentioned above, the technical quality of the documents is of crucial importance. Something which is "just okay", which is acceptable in case of a set of notes, is not acceptable for a MOOC. Depending on the nature of the textual documents, the work is extremely variable, ranging from simple formatting for an ordinary document to the drawing of graphic diagrams and illustrations. Certain complex illustrations may require more than a day of work; others an hour or less.

For the scientific domain, the writing of documents with complicated formulae may be a lengthy process. This depends heavily on the form and quality of the documents delivered by the teachers.

The working time needs to be evaluated on a case-by-case basis, and experience shows us that it is extremely variable: the preparation of the equivalent of a copy may require less than a day of work in some cases, or up to a month in others. However, the expertise of these professionals is always crucial.

2.2.5. *Integrator*

The role of the integrator is to install the documents in the MOOC platform. Therefore, they need to be very familiar with that platform on a technical level. Integrating videos and PDF documents is relatively quick and easy, but directly creating documents using the tools provided by the platform (possibly by reworking existing documents) may take longer.

For an integrator to create online quizzes for the students may require a great deal of effort – particularly on the part of the teachers, because they need to clearly explain the structure of the questions to the integrator. In extreme cases, this may take more time than simply constructing it themselves. Often, it is the teachers who perform the majority of this task of integration. However, they need a correspondent, who can easily be contacted, to guide them through the technical aspects.

If the storybook has been properly prepared, the documents carefully designed in advance and the questionnaires well thought out, the time can be brought down to between ten and twenty hours. This work, usually, is performed by the teachers or their writing assistants.

2.2.6. *Testers*

It is impossible to start up a MOOC without testers, qualified students, having thoroughly reviewed all the activities. Their role is not only to verify the quality of the material produced, but also the projected tempo, ensure that there are no points which require more time than set aside for it, and that the questionnaires serve the purpose required of them. Skipping of this step has led to humiliating failures, and whilst this type of difficulty would normally pass in a conventional course environment, on the net, it can give rise to negative publicity which is very damaging for the teacher and the institution responsible, as happened at Georgia Tech[3], with its MOOC on "Fundamentals of Online Education: Planning and Application". The students were insufficiently guided in the constitution of working groups, and the software was defective.

2.2.7. *Project manager*

The project manager coordinates the activities of the various participants and the schedule for the various modules. This role is absolutely crucial in this type of project: it is not possible to start up a MOOC without all of the documents having been integrated into the platform and the proposed path tested. Thus, the project manager needs to monitor the day-to-day running of the program to ensure that no one link in the chain unexpectedly causes holds up the whole process.

The project manager may be one of the teachers, the pedagogical engineer or a competent third party (e.g. a doctoral candidate) with knowledge of all aspects of the project. The important point here is that it is a completely separate mission for which somebody needs to be recruited, and that function needs to be taken into account in the work time of that person.

2.3. Steps involved in mounting a MOOC

We begin with the step where a teacher or a team of teachers has decided to engage in a MOOC and the project approved by the responsible authority. The storyboard has been outlined and the working time evaluated so as to budget for the human resources needed for the project. The project has been agreed to so that the university will inject the necessary resources.

3 http://chronicle.com/blogs/wired-campus/georgia-tech-and-coursera-try-to-recover-from-mooc-stumble/42167 by Steve Kolowich and http//onlinelearninginsights. wordpress. com/ 2013/02/01/how-not-to-design-a-mooc-the-disaster-at-coursera-and-how-to-fix-it by Debbie Morrison.

This step may require the drafting of a document, just as with any project.

2.3.1. *Announcements*

A MOOC needs to be announced sufficiently far in advance for communication to be possible and for students to be able to enroll. The major consortiums (*Coursera, edX*, etc.) announce their courses at least three months before the start date. They regularly communicate their forthcoming program.

This announcement is accompanied by two documents, which are made available on the consortium's portal page:

– a *syllabus* summarizing the essential points of the course, its duration, the prerequisites to follow the course and any relevant information to enable the learners to make their choices and be fully informed when they enroll;

– a "*teaser*" – a short video lasting two to four minutes, where the teachers appear, explaining the interest of the course that they are going to give.

These documents need to be created with the greatest care, because they are of crucial importance in attracting as broad an audience as possible.

What is the best way to time the announcements in relation to the project? Depending on the schedule established for its progression (see below), at a time when it is sufficiently advanced to be able to run the course on the announced start date. This choice will therefore depend on the complexity of the project. It is inconceivable to delay the start of a course on which thousands of students are enrolled, and there are examples of scathing failures because courses had commenced before it had been fully planned and tested.

The choice of date for the publication and posting online of the "teaser" is therefore crucial. Once the date has been announced, the course must indeed start on that date. This implies that all the videos must be ready. Hence, the French platform *FUN* insists that all "rushes" must have been recorded before a launch date is announced.

Step 1: the project

Bringing together the actors (teachers, support team), reaching agreement on the future course, drawing together the documentation and evaluating the required workload, takes some time. It is the time taken for storyboarding and, therefore, work with the instructional designer. Once this has been completed, it is still necessary to evaluate the amount of work required for the textual documents and collect the illustrations to be used on the course. It is therefore possible to evaluate the workload required of the support staff, graphic designers, integrators and others.

Then, we still need to plan the project in order to properly time the date of the announcements.

Step 2: production

The different documents can be created in parallel: it is not necessary for the textual documents or questionnaires to have been constructed in order for the videos to be recorded.

Let us take the typical example of a MOOC eight weeks in duration with an hour of video per week (in four to six sequences). The recording would take a total of around 32 hours, and the editing process around 240 hours. Thus, we can see that it would take over two months for an operator to complete the task. Thus, at latest, the recording process needs to begin as soon as the course is announced; preferably before.

The time it will take the teachers to write the textual documents is difficult to estimate. On the basis of various statements, we evaluate this time (although it can vary greatly as a function of the subjects), for an 8-hour filmed course, at around two weeks: 70 hours. This estimation needs to be taken with a sizeable pinch of salt, and relates to the responsibility of the authors who, often, already have documents which can serve as a starting point. This does not include the page-setting of the final document with its illustrations, which depends on the complexity of the content, the presence of equations and symbols, and the richness and number of the illustrations. The time necessary needs to be evaluated by specialists on the basis of samples. The work can be counted in days or in weeks. Certain teachers may produce final documents, and others incomplete drafts, and the workload of the integrators and graphic designers may become very heavy. Similarly, the time may vary greatly depending on the past experience and documents accumulated by the teachers on the topic of the MOOC.

Action	Weeks																			
	-n	…		-3	-2	-1	Announcement	1	2	3	4	5	6	7	8	9	10	11	12	Start
Teaser					■															
Storyboarding	■	■	■	■																
Syllabus: design					■															
Preparation of oral lectures	■	■	■	■	■	■		■	■	■	■									
Video: recording			■	■	■	■		■	■	■	■	■	■							
Video: editing			■	■	■	■		■	■	■	■	■	■	■						
Video: integration										■	■	■	■	■	■					
Documents: writing	■	■	■	■	■	■		■	■											
Documents: page-setting				■	■	■		■	■	■	■	■	■	■						
Documents: illustrations		■	■	■	■	■		■	■	■	■	■	■	■						
Integration: corpus		■	■	■	■	■		■	■											
Integration: documents			■	■	■	■		■	■	■	■	■	■	■	■					
Integration: questionnaires			■	■	■	■		■	■	■	■	■	■	■	■					
Integration: videos						■		■	■	■	■	■	■	■	■	■				
Tests										■	■	■	■	■	■	■	■			
Corrections										■	■	■	■	■	■	■	■	■		

Table 2.1. *Representative timetable for the development of a MOOC*

The above table gives a representative example of the arrangement of a project. The aim of this table is to demonstrate the complexity of the task of organizing a MOOC, and therefore the need to have a project manager. Thus, the durations shown are arbitrary, except for the video, where the times are fairly well known. Great care should be exercised when reading the table, and it should be adapted to the particular aspects of each project. Essentially, what we wish to demonstrate with this table is that preparation needs to begin long before the official announcement of the course, and it is unrealistic to attempt to put together a MOOC in less than three or four months.

We have appropriately coordinated the dates of the announcements and the start of the course. Quite deliberately, the time-periods used are extremely short: the preparation of the oral lecture begins before the end of the storyboarding, as does the recording of the first videos, because it is difficult to reduce the amount of time taken for these steps. In reality, the tasks would be less parallel, which would increase the length of time needed. However, we can see, from this theoretical example, that at least four months must be allowed. Thus, the staging of a MOOC is no mean feat!

The construction of a MOOC is a far more complex task than preparation for a conventional course, and it requires a degree of organization similar to that needed in industrial projects, which is not common in the area of education. We shall discuss this point in the next chapter.

2.4. Resources required

Given that, as we have seen, a MOOC is, first and foremost, a course and interaction, a software package is needed to edit the documents and manage the interaction. Often, one speaks of a *studio platform* to denote this tool, which serves multiple functions. This platform serves as a content editor, and it helps the design team to format the documents and insert videos and photos. The same software takes care of the interaction between teachers and learners. It provides a forum, a chatroom and various means of organizing and joining groups, and also facilitates the insertion and correction of exercises. Put simply, the software platform must be a very high-level content editor, and must facilitate sophisticated management of student/teacher interaction. As we shall see, there are a number of existing platforms specifically dedicated to MOOCs, and, as one might imagine, new ones are being developed with a view to finding a place in an expanding, diversifying market. Note, however, that certain MOOC designers have made use of existing LMSs such as *Sakai* or *Moodle* (*Modular Object-Oriented Dynamic Learning Environment*) or *Claroline*. These three platforms, which have the advantage of being in the domain of open software, already offer numerous functions to post lectures and exercises online and manage groups of students. For example, the MOOC *Courlis* was developed on *Moodle*. *Claroline*, which was originally developed at the Catholic University of Leuven, spearheaded by Marcel Lebrun, is in the process of migrating, with the help of the team at Lyon 1 who created SPIRAL and the support of the Wallonie and Rhône-Alpes regional councils, toward a new generation of LMS: *Claroline Connect*.

Numerous platforms are under development, and at present it is difficult to know which of them will achieve widespread success. Obviously, many classic e-learning platforms, such as *Moodle* or *Sakai*, will adapt to the needs of MOOCs. Also, influential actors in the field of e-learning, such as the *Open University*, develop their own tools: *FutureLearn* in the United Kingdom, and *Miriada X* in Spain. There is beginning to be an abundant range of available platforms; some require a financial contribution in return for hosting the course. For the future, we will undoubtedly see the progressive development of a range of open platforms, based on the open software model. Already, we have *OpenedX*, which is available as Open Source software (see section 4.2).

It is important not to confuse the software platform – which is crucial for the development and execution of a MOOC – with the computer infrastructure and the operating software necessary to provide a high-quality service to potentially a very high number of simultaneous users, requiring huge volumes of content. In the latter case, we speak of a *hardware platform*, even though the operating software is included (see section 2.7).

The hardware and software resources necessary to create documents other than video are commonplace. The electronic formats employed are typical: PDF, HTML, etc. It is simply necessary to have the appropriate tools and skills to make use of them (e.g. *Office, OpenOffice, Photoshop,* etc.).

For video, it is sufficient to have a fairly simple recording studio, with two cameras to film two different points of view. High definition (HD) is required. It is essential to show the speaker at the same time as the documents illustrating what is being said. This helps maintain the participants' attention. It is crucial to avoid limiting oneself to the mere projection of slides with an accompanying voice recording. It may be acceptable to simply film the professor and present accompanying slides, in law or in the humanities, for example, but is to be avoided in science, because the lecture would soon become very boring.

Better still, showing the speaker writing using a graphic tablet or a digital whiteboard will bring the student closer to the teacher. Progressively revealing handwritten notes is very impressive. In order to do so, we need to record the screen of the computer, using programs such as *Camtasia, BB FlashBack Pro 4, Screenflow* (for Mac) and many others. This is particularly true when the lecture includes diagrams and equations: the speaker can draw formulas and graphs in real time, which will make the final video more vibrant.

The cost of equipment for a good studio may be more than $30,000, but it is possible to achieve recordings of perfectly acceptable quality for far less than that[4]. This depends on the complexity of the videos we wish to make. A mathematical explanation, for example, requires more sophisticated resources than a simple speech, because it is highly instructive to show the teacher writing on a tablet or interactive whiteboard.

It is worth employing all the tricks of the trade of film-making in order to sustain the learners' attention.

---

4 Examples can be found at EPFL: "*MOOC Factory*" https://moocs.epfl.ch/page-85490-fr.html.

In terms of video editing and montage, there are numerous tools available for Macs and PCs at a reasonable price (*Final Cut, Premiere,* etc.). The cost of acquiring a studio is very soon recouped by the results. The real problem is the personnel needed to produce the film, and some teachers prefer to subcontract the work to private companies, but of course, there is a cost involved. This point is discussed in the next chapter.

In summary, a MOOC is a project which requires very diverse skills. Before diving into one, it is wise to reflect on a certain number of important points:

1) Defining the project:

- What is the course that we wish to disseminate? What are its objectives?

- Are its duration and its form appropriate for the type of MOOC we are considering?

- Who are the audience that we wish to attract?

2) Preparation of the project:

- Is the project team defined?

- Has the project manager been accepted in that role by all those involved?

- Do we have all the necessary resources at our disposal?

- What are the stages of the project: the projected schedule?

2.5. Post-construction tasks

Once a MOOC begins, the task of the production and support teams is finished. The same is not true, however, for the work of the teachers.

While the amount of interaction between learners and teachers may be reduced, it is still necessary to a certain degree. In light of the large number of participants, it is clearly not possible to correspond with each of them individually, and the platforms designed for MOOCs have integrated collaborative tools to try to overcome this problem. The learners are supposed to help one another. To that end, they can come together in spontaneous communities or groups organized as part of the MOOC, or conduct exchanges with all of the participants. This is one of the fundamental principles of a cMOOC.

The teachers tend to stay somewhat in the background, intervening to bring discussions back on track, or correct them if need be; their role is also to initiate or revisit discussions on important points. They are as much *community managers* as they are teachers. This task may be extremely demanding. They must allow for between five and ten hours per week, which may be divided between all the members of the team – the teachers and their assistants if there are any. The quality of the organization is of crucial importance for the success of the MOOC: the predefined tutorials schedule needs to be respected, and the topics to be covered in each one need to be clearly defined. Once again, because of the number of participants, it is necessary to employ a form of organization with which few teachers are familiar. Some MOOCs have proved disastrous, because the course organizers were not present in front of the students. Some MOOCs include live video streams where the participants can ask questions and make comments. They use various devices, such as chatrooms, *Twitter* or equivalent services, which are universally available: these are priceless tools for conducting live dialog. It is advisable to conduct data analysis on the students' activity, so as to be able to quickly rectify any possible errors in the course scenario.

Thus, the "*community manager*" is an essential element in ensuring the success of a MOOC. There are many MOOC designers who have been struck by the amount of work represented by that management task, which they had underestimated before starting their course.

Finally, at the end of the course, it is crucial to analyze how it has gone, and examine the students' behavior, with a view to improving the course for any future convocation and understanding the reasons behind a drop-out rate which is invariably high. Another reason is that, in the fairly near future, one can expect a dramatic evolution of

MOOC platforms, which will enable the teaching to be tailored and adapted specifically to the needs of each student. These sophisticated tools can only be employed to their full potential if we have gained an understanding of the reactions of past participants. It is now possible to envisage seeing and analyzing the mistakes made by a learner, which should, in theory, allow for personalized comments and teaching. In addition, it is essential to include a student satisfaction questionnaire in all courses… and study the responses carefully!

Quality is a *leitmotif* in MOOCs. All specialists in the field stress the need to present documents and a storyboard which are more fully developed than in a typical distance-learning course. There are at least two good reasons for this. The first is simple: it is not possible to adjust gradually, as can be done with small groups. In conventional distance learning, the one-to-one links between students and teachers compensate for this less-polished aspect, and it is possible to correct the progression of the course in real time. In a MOOC, because of the sheer mass of the participants, this becomes impossible. We lose the right to make a mistake.

The second reason for this absolute necessity for quality is that, unlike a person taking a distance-learning course through an open university, a "MOOCer" is, in principle, alone: they do not have the option to obtain extra explanations – e.g. to illustrate a concept which remains obscure or a confusing idea. We shall see later on that this solitude does, indeed, pose a real problem.

Quality control is therefore absolutely crucial, and inevitably, there is a cost associated with this.

2.6. Amount of human resources required for the construction of a MOOC

Imagine an 8-week course which, *grosso modo*, corresponds to a teaching unit of 8 hours of lectures per week, either in person or presented via video. Let us also imagine that the MOOC in question will be repeated three times. Obviously, the cost drops when a course is repeated numerous times, because whilst corrections and updates may need to be made, it is not necessary to repeat all of the preparatory work. All the calculations shown below, for all categories of staff discussed, represent the effective working time.

Beyond video, it is very difficult to reach a figure for the general cost of a MOOC, and our estimations in this section should not be taken as gospel. From one course to another, depending on the complexity of the documents needing to be prepared, the number of those documents (to write documents of one's own is something quite different to simply using documents which are already available on the Web), and whether or not it is possible to use one's own archives, the lengths of time required may vary greatly. We shall also work on the basis of the hypothesis that the teachers are not inexperienced: they have already taught the subject, or at least a similar one, in a normal classroom setting.

2.6.1. *For teachers*

The amount of time taken by the teachers to prepare a MOOC is no different to the time commitment required to prepare a conventional course, but it does vary enormously on the basis of the subject and level. We estimate the time requirement as being around 5 hours for each hour of lecture in a theater or on film, the first time, and 1 hour each time after that. In the case of filmed lectures, the teacher will need to spend around four hours in the studio per hour of film – i.e. three hours more than with a simple presentation in a lecture theater. The cost of a MOOC, therefore, is a great deal higher the first year than it is for a traditional course. For the subsequent years, the necessary updates represent around 1/3 of the initial time – i.e. 20 hours for the documents, and much less for the preparation of the oral content. The investment for a MOOC, in terms of the teaching staff's working time, can only be recouped if the course is repeated at least three times or three years running, as we shall see later on.

The time taken to write the documents is estimated on the basis of the time to write a set of notes: 90 hours for the initial version, and 20 hours for the other two times. This does not include the time needed by the support team for page-setting and illustration.

It is necessary, in a MOOC, to put measures in place for evaluation, in the form of quizzes, homework (which will be corrected not by the teachers but by the other students, unless automated correction is a possibility). We shall arbitrarily estimate this as 4 hours per week, so 32 hours for the whole course. This does not include the time needed to transfer these exercises into the quiz system used by the platform in question.

The animation of the course (by the *community manager*) corresponds to around 6 hours per week, so 48 hours in total. Note that a face-to-face course requires 4 hours of preparation per 1½-hour session of applied work. It is in this area, therefore, that a MOOC can represent a saving in terms of university education. With students working by themselves, being tested by means of quizzes and online homework, the traditional applied-work classes are replaced by less frequent meetings to make the point and follow everybody's work in a non-anonymous fashion.

A MOOC is a complex project, which involves work for a whole team of people. The contact time required is certainly at least 30 hours. This figure is higher than the time needed for consultation, face-to-face contact and panel holding in conventional teaching – times which are never counted specifically. We shall integrate it into our calculations, because this consultation is absolutely essential for the quality of a MOOC. When a MOOC includes several contributors, the times taken by each of them are added together for each participant. For simplicity's sake, we shall consider only one.

We have not counted the time taken to analyze the students' behavior, or the meetings during the course. We can consider these as being integrated into the time worked by the *community manager*. Similarly, in face-to-face teaching, we neglect the time taken for consultation and panels.

The row "Writing of corrected exercises" corresponds to the necessity, in scientific disciplines, to put exercises to the students, which are crucial in order for them to be able to assimilate the theoretical aspects, and the teacher to be able to check their comprehension. This is traditionally done in applied work classes, but in exceptional cases, teachers will give students written corrections. One usually uses a whiteboard. The writing of this document requires long and painstaking work: there can be no question of leaving any calculation error, and even less a reasoning error, which would be corrected in real time in class.

Working hours: teachers					
Task	Hours			Total	Comments
	Course 1	Course 2	Course 3		
Oral preparation	40	8	8		
Writing of documents	90	20	20		
Writing of corrected exercises	40	10	10		Optional depending on the discipline
Recording of video	32	8	8		Each session requires half a day, i.e. the time is counted in multiples of 4 hours
Preparation of quizzes and homework	32	6	6		
Preparation of the project	30	5	5		
Total	264	57	57		
Total for the preparation of the MOOC				**378**	Time which the teacher needs to devote to the construction of the MOOC
Animation MOOC	48	48	48		
Total MOOC (approximate)	312	105	105	**520**	

2.6.2. *Teaching support staff*

In this category, we shall include the work which can be entrusted to staff who are less qualified but nonetheless capable of teaching – particularly “grad” students or PhD candidates.

The testers are the people who check how well the course works before it is launched. At least two would be needed. It is to be hoped, if we choose students in the domain, that they will need less time than the *ab initio* learners. On the basis of four hours of work per week for these learners, i.e. 32 hours for the whole course, we would allow 15 hours for each tester, or 30 hours for two. This is probably an underestimation, but it is possible that these students will learn something themselves by following the course. If the testers are teachers, this figure needs to be increased.

Here, we shall include the work of the instructional designer, because this role could potentially be partially fulfilled by a teacher. Indeed, the designer must have skills in the subject, as explained in section 2.2. The task takes around 40 hours minimum, in view of the need to take part in meetings. It is wise to use the project manager for this position, thereby avoiding having to count a significant portion of the meeting hours twice.

The work of the project manager (who may be a teacher or the instructional designer) is at least 60 hours, in view of the fact that he or she takes part in some of the teachers' meetings (30 hours).

Working hours: teaching support staff				
Task	Hours			Total
	Course 1	Course 2	Course 3	
Instructional designer	40	8	8	
Project manager	60	12	12	
Testers	60	12	12	
Total	160	32	32	
Total for the MOOC (approximate)				**225**

The tests require the participation of various people, in relation to different aspects. These tests are not limited to verifying the logical progression of the objectives in the course, but also include an aspect of validation of the teaching, the examinations, the exercises and homework.

2.6.3. *Technical support staff*

Outside of the realm of video, the time periods are arbitrary, and are given, for example, on the basis of the experience gained from several MOOCs, or advanced courses on a teaching platform.

We can estimate that 8 hours of video require around 240 hours of editing and montage. This evaluation is based on our experience of putting on quality courses. The estimations given by the EPFL are similar, although slightly less because in their case, the recording is automated, with the professor moving around a studio designed specifically for the purpose, and different cameras are used . However, these post-production times also depend on the tools used. The experience gained from *Courlis*, run in Nancy, shows that with the use of *iSpring* and a studio equipped with two cameras and a rostrum camera, we are looking at 16 hours of recording and 16 hours of post-production, i.e. 32 hours, for 8 hours of video. It is certainly true that the more we reduce the time devoted to production and editing, the more the quality suffers, and increasingly, the end result begins to look like a simple filmed version of an oral lecture, without illustrations on paper, tablet or interactive whiteboard.

The time taken to format the documents is tricky to evaluate, as is the illustration, because it depends on the disciplines, the materials, and is specific to each subject. It also depends on the quality and structuring of the documents written by the teachers (we imagine they provide the technicians with these documents in electronic form). A primarily text-based course may require less than a day, but if it contains equations, it is possible to have to spend up to a week (35 hours) on it. As regards the illustrations, the time required may range from a few hours to over a month, for the same reasons. In reality, the estimation of these times will be included in the analysis phase of a project. We shall use an arbitrary estimate of 10 hours for page-setting and 35 hours for the illustrations. The preparation of the documents is the part which is most variable from one project to another. It needs to be carefully evaluated rather than underestimated. These figures should be viewed with a great deal of caution, because the time needed can vary enormously depending on the subject, the complexity of the document (equations, diagrams, images, etc.) and the capabilities of the teacher to create a high-quality document themselves. The integration of the documents onto the platform and the construction of the course will be estimated at around fifteen hours, based on our own experience.

Working hours: technical support staff				
Task	Hours			Comments
	Course 1	Course 2	Course 3	
Video recording	32	6	6	
Video editing	240	50	50	In order to be able to reuse videos from previous years, we must have the capacity to store those previous videos
Formatting of texts	10	2	2	Variable depending on the degree of skill of the teachers and the quality of the documents they produce
Illustrations	35	7	7	Variable depending on the number and complexity of the documents
Integration	15	3	3	
Participation in meetings	10	2	2	Estimation for all staff involved in the project
Total	342	70	70	
Total for the MOOC (approximate)				480

If we add together all these working hours, we arrive at a figure of around 1,200 hours (520 + 480 + 225), with a certain degree of variability (± 400 hours) depending on the players' experience and the degree of refinement of the MOOC[5].

5 Also see http://blog.educpros.fr/matthieu.cisel/2013/11/12/monter-un-mooc-combien-ça-coute.

It is evident that these estimations can vary considerably depending on the content, the form and the objectives of the course leaders. However, our experience, after having discussed the matter with the leaders of numerous MOOCs, suggests that these values are not exaggerated – and actually seem to be rather conservative.

2.7. Cost of a MOOC

2.7.1. *Logistics*

A MOOC requires both hardware and software resources in order to prepare the content. The software used is, for the most part, typical (word processing programs, *Photoshop, Illustrator*, etc.) and is very often available in universities. The same is true of the resources needed for video production, with the exception of a studio.

The cost of a studio is extremely variable: while only a few thousand dollars would be needed to film a speaker, in satisfactory conditions, with a single camera, it would take around $30,000-50,000 to build a sophisticated studio where it is possible to change the background, and record a speaker writing on an interactive whiteboard and/or a graphic tablet, from multiple points of view.

Presenting quality, lively videos, where we see the professor in action from a variety of angles, is important to maintain the learners' attention. Thus, it is important not to merely attempt to "cobble something together", but rather actually invest in this very important area. The quality of a course is often judged on the basis of this criterion, and many MOOCs have already had poor reviews because of mediocre video production.

2.7.2. *Software platform*

As we have seen, it makes better sense to have a dedicated MOOC platform than to rely on existing LMSs. The cost of use of these platforms is variable, but in general, the LMS will take a certain percentage of the revenue generated by the course, and certain platforms are in the process of being made available as open-source software, such as *edX* (see section 4.2). In any case, though, it is not reasonable for most establishments to envisage developing their own MOOC support software.

The investment needed, in terms both of material and human resources, is quite significant, and means that, except for experimental purposes to begin with, no universities can afford to risk creating their own MOOC platforms. The EPFL has not taken that risk, but uses *Coursera* and *edX* to host its courses. However, posting its MOOCs on an existing platform entails a cost, because the service provider will demand either an entry fee or a certain percentage of revenues or a charge per number of subscribers. Thus, depending on the contract, *Coursera* may take a fixed fee of several thousand dollars, plus a fixed sum per subscriber, whereas *edX* takes less of a commission per subscriber but charges a higher fixed fee. These platforms may provide users with a whole range of services, from development of the MOOC to training of the developers. These additional services, obviously, come at a price. On the other hand, the platforms *OpenedX* and *Canvas Network* are free, but the creator of the MOOC must take care of everything, from the installation of the software on their system to publicizing the course and handling the participants' registration (see section 4.2).

2.7.3. *Hardware platform*

In order to distribute courses, it is necessary to have a hardware infrastructure to host the portal via which the course is accessed, which enables the learner to follow the course comfortably, supporting the data exchanges and the software for the interaction. This computer infrastructure is moderately complex, and requires diverse skills and funding because of the high number of potential simultaneous logons. The resources necessary to serve a large number of users and guarantee good availability are only within reach of consortiums and specialized companies or to large, skilled computing firms. It is wise to research the constraints that are imposed by the hardware platform employed, but this has little impact on the requirements in terms of software tools.

The need to be able to simultaneously cater for tens of thousands of learners necessitates the installation of a set of servers capable of dealing with a workload which is extremely variable over time. It is possible to discern daily and weekly cycles in terms of level of demand. Whilst these cycles are well-documented and even are to be expected, today they are occurring on a far greater scale than ever before, which may catch the managers of LMSs unprepared. For example, when the University of Amsterdam launched its first MOOC in 2012, the simple announcement on the 8 pm news triggered a surge in demand which required the addition of a new server every hour. More recently, Rémi Bachelet, head of the MOOC "*Gestion de projet*" (Project Management) at the *Ecole Centrale de Lille*, in France, recorded extreme peaks after broadcasts on the radio or on television channels. All of this goes to show that a MOOC requires a flexible, adaptable computer architecture, capable of quickly responding to variable levels of demand. For this purpose, we need not only hardware but also virtualization systems for the servers and programs, for MOOCs, which are capable of running on such architectures.

There are two solutions. The university may choose to use its own hardware if its technicians have the necessary knowhow to construct that architecture in *IaaS* mode (*Infrastructure as a Service*). The servers can be booted up or shut down without needing to worry about the physical machines. It is necessary, in advance, to design and install machines of sufficient capacity to deal with peak loads, which requires a considerable amount of investment. Of course, the university also needs to have competent engineers to build and operate that architecture.

It is possible to run in *SaaS* mode (*Software as a Service*), using an external contractor to provide the infrastructure. In this case, all that needs to be done is to open up instances of the program which runs the MOOCs. This is the choice made by the American consortiums (*Coursera, edX, Udacity*) who make use of Amazon's AWS (*Advanced Web Services*). Thus, each course corresponds to one or more virtual programs, opened and closed dynamically. This method is extremely flexible, and the costs are calculated on the basis of the amount of use made of the service. There is no need to pay for the theoretical maximum use. The decision to use a commercial firm to provide these services is a politically risky one, because of the possibility for the LMS to collect learners' personal data.

In order to offer satisfactory access to a MOOC, systems engineers must be available to ensure the continuity of the service. Their role is to ensure the sustainability of the service, to deal with any incident that occurs and to find quick workarounds for bugs and solutions to all the inevitable difficulties. In addition to these purely computing staff, pedagogical engineers need to have profound knowledge of the software in order to deal with the demand for help from the professors creating the courses, to write and update the documents and, more generally, monitor the application functions.

Finally, the whole lifecycle of the courses needs to be attended to: creation and granting of rights to the professors, publication to make them available to the students, closure, etc. Put simply, an appropriate administrative framework needs to be established.

2.7.4. *Human resources*

When we look at the above points and tables, we can see that the cost of a MOOC, from the point of view of the teachers, assuming that the course is repeated three times, is only truly greater than that of a conventional course if the professor does not provide notes and if there is only one applied work group. A course or a training program must be repeated in order to justify the investment injected into a MOOC; here we make the hypothesis that the course is taught at least three times. We also suppose that the MOOC renders the applied work classes either partly or completely obsolete, because the students can, and do, practise online. Thus, with two groups, the costs become equivalent. This limit is arbitrary, because the variability of the estimations with subject matters and disciplines means that it may change dramatically. It is indisputable that, when the number of applied work groups increases, the balance quickly tips in favor of a MOOC. Thus, for a professor teaching the same course three years running (with certain adjustments every year) and taking charge of two applied work groups, a MOOC is more or less the same in terms of the workload it represents.

The excess cost becomes apparent in the area of teacher support (engineers, project manager, testers) and technical support. In our estimation, this represents around 700 hours, with all categories agglomerated.

These calculations may be modified, in light of a variety of factors which can be taken into consideration:

1) If a MOOC is used as a SPOC (*Small, Private, On-line Course*), i.e. as an online course restricted to the regular students of a course (see section 1.3), it is also necessary to add the time taken for face-to-face classes with the students to focus on points of interest and deal with any personal difficulties they may be having. A one-hour applied lecture actually represents 4 hours of work. At best, one hour's face-to-face class would correspond to two hours of work. This pushes up the profit threshold of a MOOC, but nevertheless it is undeniable that in the case of units with large numbers of students, such as those dispensed in the first year of university, the excess cost represented by a MOOC is offset by the number of applied working groups.

2) If we wish to count the cost in real terms, we need to add the cost of seminar rooms and lecture theaters. In that case, the balance immediately tips in favor of a MOOC. A university which introduces a blended learning unit, partially based on MOOCs, makes a saving in terms of the cost of construction and overhead costs of the buildings.

We can therefore ask a team of teachers to switch from giving a traditional classroom-based course to giving a partly distance-learning course, based on one or more MOOCs, without consideration of their working hours, provided one agrees to maintain that course over a minimum period of three years, if not more. As the custom is to keep a course running for five years, this should be no problem for the teachers. The enormous amount of extra work needed during the first year actually represents an investment for the subsequent years.

On the other hand, a university which decides to launch a MOOC only for external students needs to find the full amount of funding:

– over 300 teacher hours for the first time the course is run, and 110 hours the subsequent times;

– 160 hours of teacher support for the first year, and 30 hours the subsequent times;

– 340 hours of technical support in the first year, and 70 in the next two years.

The launching of a MOOC worldwide is therefore an operation for which a university needs to find funding which is difficult to justify in the education budget. This action can be presented as a communication operation, an operation to draw in foreign students, or any other way, but certainly cannot be free.

The table below shows the costs incurred on the basis of a cost of $6,500/month for teaching and support staff, and $5,000 for technical support. The figures are approximated, in view of the degree of accuracy of the estimations. They include only the salaries and employee contributions, but not the overheads attached to the working environment.

Cost of human resources				
	Year 1	Year 2	Year 3	Total for the MOOC
Teachers	20,000	7,000	7,000	
Teaching support staff	8,000	2,000	2,000	
Technical support	13,000	2,500	2,500	
Total	41,000	11,500	11,500	
Total cost (approximate)				$64,000

It should once again be stressed that these figures are extremely approximate:

1) The preparation time taken by the teachers can vary enormously depending on the subject, the authors' experience and the documents they already have available (it is unlikely that anyone would attempt to construct a MOOC on a subject which they had not already gained practical experience teaching).

2) In calculating the cost of the work of technical support, we assume that the staff are really employed full-time. This is true, in particular, for the video technicians. Possibly, not all universities have need of full-time employees in this area, and will have to contract the

work out to private providers. The true cost of an hour, integrating all activities other than the time spent on recording and editing, is not taken into account.

3) There is a significant degree of variety in the total amount of work required for each MOOC, depending on the subject and the amount of illustration support.

Thus, assuming the software and hardware platforms are at our disposal, the cost of a MOOC is at least $30,000 for course with little animation (e.g. in law) and may reach up to $60,000 for particularly sophisticated courses in the area of sciences. To compare it to a conventional course, when we wish to use it essentially for internal training (i.e. a SPOC), we also need to add the cost of applied lecture groups and the overheads for the running of the premises. A MOOC can only be financially viable if it is taken by large numbers of students, such as those in the first few years of university. Yet it would be very reductive to limit ourselves only to this utilitarian approach. The pedagogical uses must not be forgotten. The testimony from MOOC designers suggest our estimations are relatively accurate, because they report costs which are usually in the range of $35,000-$50,000 in marginal costs and $200,000-$300,000 in consolidated costs, including what is need to offset the outlay for the necessary resources (studio, platforms, premises, etc.).

To conclude this summary, it is necessary to examine for whom a MOOC has been constructed for and what results can be expected. It is this that we shall discuss in the next chapter.

3

A MOOC for Whom and for What Purposes?

3.1. Audiences

A priori, there is no limitation to the domain of MOOCs: they can range from training in Java programming to a MOOC on the Siege of Yorktown or breadfruit cultivation in the Marshall Islands. There are no boundaries or limits. There is no set level either – it may just as well be addressed to primary school children as to doctoral candidates.

A MOOC on the art of fly fishing may attract a large audience of anglers; another about investment in Florida or Morocco a large audience of retirees; another on the history of the War of Independence could be very useful in primary schools. There is no age or social category which is beyond the reach of MOOCs. MOOCs are open to all audiences who wish to acquire knowledge without paying and outside of an organized system. MOOCs are particularly interesting for audiences who do not tend to meet up in their normal lives, either because they are geographically far apart or because they do not like conventional education. It is said that the best grade obtained on Sebastian Thrun's MOOC on AI was obtained by a 50-year-old housewife with no higher education!

Originally, the target audience was one of university students, but that target rapidly expanded. The philosophy behind a MOOC is to render all knowledge accessible, without any geographical or social boundaries. Thus, today, MOOCs are attracting students and professionals in search of training alike, or inactive people (be it for voluntary or involuntary reasons) wishing to improve their level of language, computer skills, etc. It should certainly be noted that the typical audience for a MOOC is over 28 years of age and is not enrolled in higher education.

In addition, one of the areas targeted by MOOCs is international education – particularly Africa, south-western Asia and Latin America: all areas where there is a yawning chasm between demand and supply of higher education. For example, one of the declared objectives of the MOOCs offered by the EPFL is to attract a large number of French language speakers, as stated by Patrick Aebischer, President of EPFL, who took a sabbatical year precisely to work on MOOCs. In his opinion, rather than completely turning the university scene on its head, MOOCs serve to help reach new audiences. Thus, EPFL has already posted a number of MOOCs addressed to French speakers in southern countries: "*planification urbaine*" (urban planning) and "*informatique industrielle*" (industrial computer science), for instance. Already, the cohort of users of major LMSs such as *Coursera* and *edX* is highly international. For its part, the *Agence universitaire de la francophonie* (AUF – University French-language Agency) is also making the transition between the conventional distance-learning courses it traditionally offers and MOOCs to reach the French-speaking audience all over the world.

3.1.1. *MOOCs at university*

The best-known LMSs are driven by universities: such is the case of *edX*, which is a foundation created by a partnership between Harvard and MIT. Up until now, the courses distributed by *edX* have mainly been given by MIT, Harvard, Berkeley, Stanford and a few universities from elsewhere in the world. There are various ways to consider MOOCs in universities: MOOCs to spread the reputation of the establishment, MOOCs for the students integrated into the pedagogical models, leveling MOOCs, etc.

However, typical students, who are fairly young, manifest the desire to have a fairly vibrant social life. The idea of studying from home inspires little enthusiasm: students want to be able to meet, have exchanges, share knowledge and experiences. Nonetheless, MOOCs can be used by students as part of their "normal" course. For example, the University of Sydney, where classes are recorded, noted that after two or three weeks, students stop going to the face-to-face classes, because they prefer to listen at their own convenience, how and whenever they wish. In parallel, over the past three years, that university's library has seen a 20% reduction, each year, in the number of books borrowed, but a similar 20% increase per year in the number of students present in the library. This means that the students are going to the library for something else other than to borrow books: they need a space to share the information they have collected at home. Similarly, EPFL is investing massively in the development of MOOCs for its first-year students. For the time being, they have the choice of whether to attend the face-to-face lectures in the theater or follow the MOOC remotely; if they choose the MOOC, they can still be present on campus for practical work and applied work, to ask questions of the professor, etc. To develop its MOOCs, EPFL has created a "*MOOC Factory*", which is a model of the genre. The *MOOC factory* is a department in the university, comprising at least ten people, where professors wishing to stage a MOOC have access to a studio, and personnel skilled in recording, editing, etc. to relieve the MOOC organizer of all tasks not relating to the handling of the content and the teaching of the MOOC in question. We saw in the previous chapter that many large universities already have an online education department or a multimedia department, often staffed by ten or so people, which, if given the right tools, could constitute a solid base upon which to build a MOOC factory.

3.1.2. *Lifelong learning*

MOOCs, which represent a way to obtain certification, open up new opportunities for continuing education, which is why businesses have been attracted by the idea of MOOCs. We can point to the example of a start-up such as *Udemy*, which launched MOOC interfaces for businesses. The success of MOOCs is attributable, in particular, to the freedom they give employees to learn at their own pace, when it suits them, about topics which are of interest to them. Figures show that, often, MOOC users are executives seeking to stay abreast of the state of the art, who may not necessarily have the time to take more traditional training courses. From the point of view of a business, the advantage of MOOCs is that they enable employees to learn on their own but also collectively, as and when required. Beyond a doubt, corporate training is a fertile market for MOOCs.

On the other hand, MOOCs are directed at all the new audience groups for which traditional university education is unable to fully cater: the disabled, those in continuing education, the retired, people who can take classes at 11 o'clock at night but not during the day, because they have to work and cannot take continuing education in a specialized institution because it is too difficult to fit around their work and family commitments.

Whilst the audiences for MOOCs are very varied, the same is true of those who design them. Universities do not have a monopoly on the creation and (especially) the diffusion of knowledge and, with that in mind, we can apply the term "educational revolution". The issue remains of how to evaluate the quality of the MOOC. At present, it seems to be up to the public to assess the value of the MOOC as best they can. However, soon, online rating and reviewing (as used for restaurants and hotels, for example) are likely to provide interesting information about the value of MOOCs. Even at this stage, *Coursera* attaches a sort of stamp of quality to everything that it puts online. Very soon, we will find ourselves with many MOOCs whose value is very unequal (as, of course, is also true of conventional university courses). Social networks and potential employers will certainly differentiate between qualifications of varying degrees of worthiness. Obviously, when a higher education institution attaches value to the certificate awarded by a MOOC (e.g. by awarding university credits or re-evaluation of an employee's position, in a company), we can assume that the institution has, previously, evaluated the quality of the MOOC.

3.2. Proper use of MOOCs

3.2.1. *MOOCs as instruments of communication*

The impact of a MOOC, in terms of communication, is very significant. The primary objective for a university – for most of the members of the LERU (League of European Research Universities) – is to buoy up or maintain its reputation and ranking on the international scale, although neither Oxford nor Cambridge have acquired a presence on Britain's MOOC portal, *FutureLearn*. On the other hand, all the major American universities, which have signed up to *iTunes U*, immediately established a policy in this area, given the relevant financial backing. Both these observations are contained in the recent report published by the *Babson Survey Research Group* [ALL 14]:

1) the primary motivation for organizing a MOOC is to enhance the establishment's visibility;

2) the major universities are at the forefront in developing MOOCs.

Obviously, it is gratifying for an institution to have the most popular course in the world – in the area of Artificial Intelligence for Stanford; Mechanics for MIT; Oceanography for the Scripps Institution (part of the University of San Diego). The advantage in terms of image and prestige is clear for all to see. On the understanding that it does not negatively impact the students at the institutions in question, the hope is to attract excellent students from all over the world. Ultimately, a successful MOOC represents focused and long-lasting publicity, which, from a financial point of view, is not hugely expensive.

Coursera, the for-profit consortium based in the United States, aims to select the best courses, presented by the best teachers, at the best universities. The consortium provides its services to the world's best universities, and to them alone, for free, but takes a percentage of the revenue. Most institutions belonging to LERU have been attracted by the tactic: they all host at least a portion of their MOOCs with *Coursera*, firstly for the prestige attached to the name, and secondly because *edX* insists on a certain financial contribution. Thus, even for universities which have no ambition to "play in the big leagues", MOOCs are a useful instrument for promotion.

The major American universities, with the help of *Coursera*, wish to establish international standards: in the same way that certain books have become authoritative references for education all over the world, their aim is to deliver courses which can then be repeated elsewhere. However, there is one significant difference here: reference works, by inspiring other teachers, enable them to use the information to create their own original courses. The same will no longer be true when all the constitutive elements of a course are available "off the shelf", so that universities need only purchase them and make them available to the students. The same course, developed at Harvard or Stanford, translated into the local language, could cheaply replace a professional teacher at local level. Only a poorly-paid "*Teaching Assistant*" position would remain, locally; their only role would be to regularly provide face-to-face support to the learners enrolled at the particular institution. Certain universities, of lesser repute or whose teaching staff do not have all the necessary skills, could be tempted to adopt this strategy, or even be obliged to for financial reasons.

MOOCs can also be designed to expand the recruitment basin for potential students. American universities are particularly conscious of this issue: student recruitment is their second most prevalent motivation, according to the *Babson Survey Research Group* (*op. cit.*). Some universities offer scholarships to some of the most successful participants from their MOOCs, so one of the stated aims of EPFL is to expand its recruitment pool to include French-speaking Africa. It is certainly true that hearing that an establishment offers MOOCs will be an important deciding factor for students from abroad.

By the end of 2014, prestigious universities which do not offer MOOCs of their own are likely to be exceptions rather than the norm. A further reason for this is that developing a MOOC is a way of getting to know how the game (of higher education) is played in international spheres, and staying in the big leagues[1]. The choice of LMSs to host the MOOCs will be a political decision. The elite universities which have access to *Coursera* will use it to host some courses. Nevertheless, they may also offer courses hosted on other LMSs, again for political reasons: choice of language, national preferences (*FutureLearn*, founded by the *Open University*, tends to be used by British institutions; *Iversity* serves the same function for German universities, and *FUN* for French ones). Thus, those French institutions which have opted to use *Coursera* have all announced that they would also be putting their MOOCs on *FUN*. As regards *FutureLearn*, which is the MOOC portal used by over 20 British universities, it should be noted that it is not used by the most prestigious institutions such as Cambridge, Oxford and Imperial College, probably for reasons of image.

3.2.2. *MOOCs, distance learning and initial training*

MOOCs, in the form of SPOCs, will help to introduce support courses on a large scale:

– upon starting university, organizing refresher courses, before or at the start of the academic year;

– during the second semester, for students who have failed their exams and have to re-take them at a subsequent session in June. For universities which do not have the human resources to support these students, MOOCs can help them to work more effectively than they would be able to alone;

– they would also benefit students who have missed a few teaching units and are continuing their course;

– during the courses – especially at the start of a Masters – to help students who have joined from other courses to acquire the fundamental concepts they need in order to follow their current course. Thus, ENS in Paris is envisaging the use of MOOCs as

1 Argument put forward by Bernard Ramanantsoa, the head of HEC (Paris), interviewed by Olivier Rollot: http://orientation.blog.lemonde.fr/2013/12/11/bernard-ramanantsoa-hec-pourquoi-nous-lancons-nos-moocs/.

to bring foreign students, recruited onto its Masters programs, up to speed. At HEC in Paris, they are investigating the possibility of delivering the basics for certain courses in this way, thereby relieving the teacher of the need to painstakingly recap numerous times.

In reality, this was already possible with online LMSs which deliver the functions necessary for a SPOC. However, this usage has been hampered by the inertia of the universities which, with the exception of specific open distance-learning courses, have difficulties in integrating distance-learning parts into a mixed course. One of the problems was how, in a course which is planned to advance at a set pace, week by week, with lectures and applied-work classes, to introduce self-contained knowledge (or content) which has been prepared by somebody from off campus. Another was how the various departments would take account of this new form of teaching, which requires much more work and is much more complex, in the teachers' salaries.

This issue of the marrying of digital technology with conventional learning courses is generally met with little acceptance; yet it is an extremely important goal for the future of education. Will teachers begin to use MOOCs "done elsewhere"? Will professors weave threads from MOOCs offered by other institutions into their own courses? (This technique is known as "chunk wrapping", with "chunks" from the foreign MOOCs being "wrapped" in the fabric of the professors' own courses). More generally, there exists a large and recent reflexion about "unbundling higher education" to facilitate competition (see Presidential Innovation Papers on the site http://www.acenet.edu/PIL). The question is an important one, because on the one hand, there can be no doubt that to do so would improve certain units, but on the other, the issue of usage rights arises, and psychological barriers to the use of external content appear. Another alternative is for the teacher to recommend a MOOC as a prerequisite for their course, or as a useful extension to it. Professors certainly recommend a great many books and digital documents in their courses, and sometimes even base the end-of-unit exam partly on that content. Why not do the same with MOOCs?

In spite of these predictable bumps in the road, we can see that the impact of MOOCs is likely to force universities to change, because of "word of mouth" within the student community. How can we ignore a comment made by a student, indicating that such-and-such a MOOC, which they took with a classmate, very clearly explains (or illustrates) the part of the course which has just been covered (perhaps imperfectly)? If we follow this line of thought, it can be hoped that the distinction between face-to-face and distance learning will gradually disappear. All courses will have to include a distance-learning part. Depending on the subjects, and on the students' availability and goals, the balance may shift from a course given entirely on a face-to-face basis toward one imparted solely on a distance-learning basis. Also, as is noted by the president of the *Université de Lille 1*, Philippe Rollet, around 40% of enrolled students at that university cannot pursue their studies full time[2], usually because they have to work part-time in order to finance their studies. For these students, courses which can be taken on a distance basis are considerably helpful, and for that reason, at *Lille 1*, the whole of the undergraduate degree program is to be put online with *Unisciel*[3].

MOOCs will drastically upset the typical structure of the academic year and the organization of courses. Students will come for one-off classes, combine courses as they wish, and construct a profile for themselves, irrespective of the prospectus and without reference to a traditional qualification. A MOOC will be characterized not only by its subject but also by the university which put it online. Some students are already showing indications of this in their curriculum choices.

Particularly for distance learning, this may mean the end of qualification-awarding as we know it (for degrees and even for Masters), with the certificates being replaced by profiles detailing the units of teaching taken. Depending on their intentions, their chosen future career or their course, students will construct a portfolio which matches their objectives. In particular, distance learning courses must no longer be built on the model of face-to-face teaching, based on

2 http://www.letudiant.fr/educpros/enquetes/portrait-d-universite-numerique.

3 http://www.unisciel.fr.

complete units of teaching and university semesters, but on the building of a skills portfolio.

3.2.3. *MOOCs and continuing education*

MOOCs, in the form of SPOCs, with personalized support, are also likely to cause an upset in continuing education. The use of distance learning will become more widespread, and significant savings can be made by reducing the need for teachers to move around. It is becoming possible to construct bespoke courses, corresponding to the needs of a given business, by quickly drawing together elements based on libraries of "*learning objects*", in a prospectus or bought. The organization of courses will become easier, because a course can begin at any time, at the request of the client – not to mention the savings made by businesses, which will probably encourage their employees to study part-time outside of their working hours. Refresher courses will develop, aimed at people involved in working life who do not have a great deal of time to attend face-to-face classes – e.g. doctors, teachers, computer technicians, etc. In addition, because of their level of education, these people are able to make the most of these opportunities to bring their knowledge up to date.

The whole economy of continuing education will be upset by this – both for the sellers and buyers (providers and receivers). An important issue remains – one that is particularly important in continuing education: how to evaluate the skills and knowledge that have actually been acquired when the course comes to an end. It is this issue that we shall now go on to examine.

3.3. Assessment of learners and certification

The question of the *assessment* of learners and, *a fortiori*, that of the awarding of a certification or higher qualification, inspires a deal of lively debate. Is a simple evaluation enough? Robert Sedgewick, whose course on algorithms, given on *Coursera*, was tested by 150,000 subscribers, 50,000 of whom followed the course to completion, quite rightly points out that one would not give a reading certificate to someone who has merely bought a coursebook! Thus, there are those who oppose the idea of any organized form of assessment which, in their view, would negate the munificent idea of free and unfettered education for all.

Most likely, the position regarding assessment will depend on the type of MOOC. Somebody taking a MOOC on Italian Renaissance painting probably does not urgently need a certificate. On the other hand, somebody taking a MOOC on underwater welding, with a view to applying for a more highly-skilled job than their current one, will undoubtedly need an attestation of successful completion of the course. In the context of vocational training, the issue soon arises of the reality of knowledge acquisition: in other words, whether and how to award certification. What type of certificate should be awarded by MOOCs? Amongst other issues, there is the need to be certain that the person who has taken the MOOC is actually the person to whom the certificate is to be issued. At this stage, we should also point out a significant regulatory difficulty in relation to vocational training: often, those funding the course – e.g. aiding the unemployed to return to the job market (particularly government agencies) – will ask to see a certificate of attendance. How can we issue a certificate of attendance to someone taking a distance-learning course (MOOC)? Probably, the best thing to do would be to replace the certificate of attendance with a certificate of having followed the MOOC to completion.

If there is to be certification, should the assessment be done online or “in the flesh”? For a university MOOC, can it be open to all or should it be restricted to only those students enrolled at that university? What value can we attach to certification awarded to distance-learning students? Will certification become more prevalent than actual graduation? The answers to all these questions divide everybody, and have consequences for the place of MOOCs in education. Remember that online assessment is done comparing students’ responses to quizzes, questions and exercises to those contained in the database of the MOOC. It is also possible to assess the speed at which the students answer the questions, and their work rate.

One of the reasons why graduation from MOOCs is still such a burning issue is that, at present, there is no way for the technology to ensure, *en masse*, that the person doing the exercises online is actually the person registered on the course, or that the student does not have somebody better qualified beside him or her, whispering the answers. Distance proctoring cannot be used for everybody. The only 100% reliable solution is physical presence in the exam hall.

However, *Coursera*, for instance, awards a certification to participants who have successfully completed the MOOC and the accompanying exercises. On one level, this is a simple certification of the person's having completed the course without their identity having been verified. At the next level, *Coursera* builds up a signature for the person by means of their pace and pattern of keystrokes, and takes photos, during the tests, via the student's webcam. This is known as "signature track certification". Depending on the level of guarantee represented by the certificate, its cost ranges from less than $100 to over $300, varying with the course and the type of certificate. The maximum price is reached when the student takes a conventional examination, in person with supervision, organized by the education services company *Pearson International* – a company which already has over 150 test centers worldwide. *Coursera*'s directors state that they arc ablc to quickly set up an examination that would enable quality-control to be undertaken from home, equivalent to face-to-face exams. They estimate that the camera and the keystroke signature track already provide a sufficient level of security which can only be fooled by expert cheats – no more or less reliable than standard exams held by universities, in view of the rate of fraud. Many universities, such as Georgia Tech with its program "*Online Master's in Computer Science*", already offer academic credits (the program is not free: it costs an average of $7,000 a year). Meanwhile, *Coursera*[4] is beginning to consider offering packages of mutually-coherent MOOCs, and awarding certifications for these coherent sets of courses, which begin to resemble the courses offered by ordinary universities.

4 https://www.edsurge.com/n/2014-01-21-coursera-creates-specialization-programs-for-high-demand-subjects.

Many institutions offer a two-tier price (normal and premium) depending on the degree of reliability of the certification. A number of American universities, including MIT and Georgia Tech, have already agreed to integrate these certificates as a unit in their courses. Incoming students may be excused from taking certain classes depending on their successful completion of certain accredited MOOCs (e.g. at the University of California, Irvine; Duke University; University of Oklahoma; and the University of Pennsylvania). Depending on the university, the student will pay signature track fees, and the exam will thus be conducted securely. In certain cases, the student simply pays normal tuition fees. However, the course will remain open to non-enrolled students, as happens at the University of Oklahoma. The transfer of credits between institutions in the United States is made possible by the American Council of Education (ACE) Credit Recommendation. Generally, in order to obtain ACE-certified credits, students must take a secure examination – e.g. on online exam secured by ProctorU, or an exam taken in the flesh with Pearson International – and pay a signature track fee. Other institutions, such as Stanford, merely offer a "Statement of Accomplishment", but this certificate is free. Remember that in some American universities, there is a tradition of constructing the course, taught to their freshman students, around their pre-existing knowledge. This helps keep enrolment costs down. In Europe, the LERU recommends the exchange of MOOCs and ECTS (European Credit Transfer and Accumulation System) between participating universities to facilitate student mobility within Europe. Thus, a student working at a given university *x* can acquire a unit of value for a university *y*, where he/she could study the following year. Obviously, those who are not enrolled students at the university offering the MOOC cannot obtain a degree by taking one or more MOOCs. However, they may be issued a certificate – usually for a fee – if they have followed the whole of the course and successfully completed the exercises.

Some universities are beginning to develop a hybridized model combining MOOC elements and conventional class elements: enrollment in the MOOC is free, but at the end of the course, the students have the option to take a standard exam to validate their studies in the context of a normal course. Such is the case with the

Université de Lorraine, with its MOOC "*Courlis*" which awards a university degree when successfully completed. In order to obtain this degree, the student must undergo an exam in the flesh, which costs $250. However, it would take a very large number of students registering for the exams to cover the cost of developing a MOOC.

As an alternative to distance-evaluation or face-to-face assessment by teachers, some are also considering the option of peer assessment – i.e. assessment by other students on the same MOOC. As students tend to be quite harsh with each other, when working to hand in an essay or a report, the idea is perhaps not as far-fetched as it might sound.

Finally, it is important to acknowledge the amount of constraint attached to the workload necessary to earn the certification. On this point, we find a clear distinction between cMOOCs and xMOOCs: cMOOCs are not hugely stressful, because each individual participant can consult a particular piece of the course content whenever he or she sees fit, with varying perspectives. On the other hand, xMOOCs are rather more demanding: they require the submission of several pieces of assessed work, greater availability and the ability to keep up with the set pace in order to obtain certification. Experience has shown that with large MOOCs, the number of people diligently following the course to its completion is, at most, around 20% of the number of students who enroll at the beginning (see the next section). Thus, in the following of MOOCs, there is a widespread practice of "dipping in" to test the waters. Indeed, this is a perfectly acceptable use of MOOCs for people of any age looking to find where their own interests lie. These days, it is often the case that enrollment for the first year of a university degree is a "taster". A brief overview of MOOCs beforehand might help some school-leavers making a mistake and thereby wasting a year.

In any case, the problem of certification is far from fully resolved, although it is part of the economic model of all the actors involved, because typically, students take the MOOC for free but pay for registration for the certificate. However, as indicated previously, it is clear that the issue of assessment arises in different terms depending on the type of MOOC.

3.4. Following of MOOCs and "tutored" MOOCs

Occupational psychology tells us that in order to work well, it is best to know for whom and why we are working. MOOCs are no exception to this aspect of human psychology (see [MAC 88]). This is a point which we have not yet touched upon: the ultimate solitude of a "MOOCer"! From this standpoint, a "MOOCer" is indeed alone, and it is known that very strong motivation is needed to complete a course in such circumstances. It takes a degree of initial motivation to watch videos alone, and then what are we to do if we have not understood? It is not enough to simply rewatch a video over and over again to suddenly "see the light": whilst the ability to do this is one of the advantages of MOOCs over conventional courses, it does not compensate for the lack of immediate interaction with a teacher to whom we can explain what it is we do not understand [CHO 14]. The point could be made that the MOOCer is not really alone; that it is the role of the community and the forums to overcome this solitude. Undoubtedly, this is an effective compensation for some MOOCers: likely those who are already involved in networks. Even at this stage, MOOCers using a portal can go to *meetups* in their local communities. Thus, Coursera already has around 4,000 local communities. However, it should not be forgotten that someone with a low level of motivation, who does not know who will be looking at their work is not a good candidate for any MOOCs. This psychological aspect of the courses is an additional argument to suggest that people more mature than the average student are much more likely to be "clients" for MOOCs and to diligently follow the program.

In a MOOC, students do not have the direct support of their teachers, but they do have the support of all the other students partaking of the same session. The presence of the teacher is replaced by the emulation found in the forum; there is also real-time assessment of the exercises which can, in some ways, be similar to video games, which creates a sense of addiction. Yet all these compensations seem insufficient to retain the attention of someone who, for personal or professional reasons, is not highly motivated (which is indeed the case for most young students – as we shall see later on, this is one of the limitations of MOOCs at university. As Karsenti [KAR 13] points out, whether with a MOOC or a typical course: “rare are those students who will go further in terms of participation than what is required of them. If they are graded for three contributions to the course forum, they will make three contributions and no more”[5].

A MOOC is an interactive book. Yet as we know, for many people, it is not enough to simply give them a book in order for them to learn. In addition, the dropout rates recorded by MOOC operators are always higher than 80%. MIT says that only 10-15% of enrolled students actually finish the MOOCs. Owen Youngman, who posted the first MOOC at Northwestern University on “*Understanding media by understanding Google*”, gives the following figures, which offer quite an accurate representation of the situation: out of 55,000 enrolled students, 19,000 will actually begin the course, only 2,400 complete all the exercises and 1,196 obtain the certificate. Recent studies, such as that published on the Website of Britain’s *Open University*, reports than on average, 7% of those who sign up for the course actually pursue it to the end. Lower figures, of around 5%, are given by the *Pennsylvania Graduate School of Education*, with a peak rate of abandonment during the second week of the course. The aforementioned SCALA course, given by EPFL, is one of the frontrunners, with less than 80% of registered students dropping out. We can summarize the situation, saying that around 85% of registered students either never start the course or drop it very soon, and only 5-10% actually complete the course and are eligible for the “Statement of Accomplishment” awarded by Stanford or the “Signature track certification” given by *Coursera*. It should be noted, though, that of those people who actually pay for enrolment in a “signature track” program, the rate of completion is 90%. Another way of increasing the completion rate is to better target the audience for the MOOC, and clearly advertise the subject and level of the MOOC; in this case, the

5 Original French: “*rares sont les étudiants qui participeront au-delà de ce qui leur est demandé. S’ils sont notés pour trois interventions sur le forum du cours, ils en feront trois*”.

completion rate rises from 3 to 7%, in the experience of a course in mechanics from MIT, taught by David Pritchard (see [HOL 14], p. 42). Many MOOCs attempt to collect data about the participants after they have finished the course. If this survey were to be conducted before the start of the course – i.e. if, in order to enroll for the MOOC, students had to provide a certain amount of personal information about their level, background, motivation, etc. – then of those who have filled in that preliminary survey, the completion rate climbs above 15% (18% in one experiment given at Cuyahoga Community College ([HOL 14], p. 129)).

Indeed, it is not clear exactly why participants drop out. There have been no studies conducted on this subject. Besides the difficulties mentioned above (the level of the course and lack of prerequisites, lack of availability for the necessary workload, etc.), perhaps some participants join simply to have a look around, and leave once they are satisfied with the information they have acquired. Hence, a MOOC is an *à la carte* menu.

If we wish to increase the pedagogical effectiveness of MOOCs, probably a good tactic would be to rethink distance learning, providing MOOCers with human support to compensate for the absence of a teacher. Indeed, in a MOOC, the professor/designer disappears once the course is online; in certain cases, they may continue to make contributions via chats or the forum, but the question remains of who takes over at a human level. There are two possible answers to this: either the baton is taken up by the community or the designer arranges a support system, involving auxiliary teaching staff, who could be called “teaching assistants” in a university context, but whom we can generally call “*tutors*”.

As it transpires, we already have experience of tutored online learning. In old-style distance learning by mail, it was tutors who corrected students’ notes and sent them guidance. Consider the experience of the first-year course in Medicine at the University of Grenoble where – as we saw in our discussion of the history of the discipline – the teaching which was originally distributed on DVD has, since 2006, gradually transformed into a true MOOC. The principle adopted is that the students follow the online units from wherever they wish, but at a set pace, as happens with most MOOCs, and then have practical work sessions and/or exercises and Q&A sessions with a teacher or a final-year Medicine student. These sessions are known as "face-to-face interactive complementary classes" (FICCs). We can now view this experience with a fair amount of distance and objectivity/perspective (P. Gillois[6] *et al.* [GIL 13]). The results of the study show significant adhesion both among teachers (100% favorable) and students (satisfaction rate higher than 85%). Whilst there is a noted drop of attendance at FICCs, it is encouraging to see that the results gained by the students in the competitive exams correlate exactly to the students participating in these sessions. Moreover, the elimination of the formal lecture format and the introduction of the accompanying educational reform, with a forum, FICCs and tutors led to an increase in the success rate of students of a less fortunate social background, incontestably proving the possibility that online learning, forums and tutoring increase the accessibility of education, and help to make it more widespread.

This improvement in students' performance – particularly that of the less advantaged students – is also indicated by many other experiments. We can cite the particular experiment of Professor Michael Cima[7], who teaches Chemistry at MIT (see [HOL 14], case 6 and the references therein), who delivered his class in the form of a MOOC and then compared the outcome with that of previous years. An essential point in his experiment is the "weekly assessments" which the students have to take, in supervised exam rooms. As in the case of Grenoble, either before or after their assessment, a teaching assistant (TA) is made available to the students to answer any questions they may have. Michael Cima's conclusions are clear: the students' performance improves; they praise the use of weekly assessments, and make extensive use of the 11 TAs involved in the

6 http://www.em-consulte.com/revue/lpm; also see the lecture by Daniel Pagonis: http://tice.univ-paris1.fr/29905392/0/ficheactualite/&RH=wtice_videoblog&RF=wtice_videoblog.

7 http://web.mit.edu/fnl/volume/261/cima.html.

experiment. The flip-side of the coin is that the cost of this course is significantly higher than that of a conventional course.

Similarly, Khosrow Ghadiri, from San José State University, in his course "Introduction to Circuit Analysis" (see [HOL 14], case 7 and the references therein) speaks of a very significant improvement in students' performances – particularly those of the weaker students. As with the previous experiments, the system employed by Ghadiri is the "flipped-classroom" method: i.e. there are still in-class sessions for giving explanations on the most difficult concepts as ranked by the students. Many in-class assessments were also organized throughout the semester. The majority of students appreciate this new system, although it requires more work and greater availability than a conventional course.

In the same vein, the online university WGU (http://www.wgu.edu/admissions/academic_experience_mentor) automatically dedicates a guide, called mentor, to support each student throughout their academic career and asks: "isn't mentoring an essential faculty role?".

Other experiments in distance learning, such as the teaching of first-year Medicine in New Caledonia offered by UPMC, or the teaching of ultrasound techniques in Senegal, performed by the UNF3S (Digital French-Language University of Health Sciences and Sport), illustrate that a human presence in addition to online teaching considerably increases the impact and the success rate of these courses. In the MOOC *Eurêka*, designed for junior-high school students and delivered with Unisciel (see section 2.2), there is also the possibility of sending tutors into high schools to deliver support and encouragement alongside the MOOC. Generally, these tutors will be students at a university of technology.

With the ultrasound experiment, it was teachers at the University of Dakar who supervised the practical work. In Grenoble, third-year Medicine students "tutor" the first-year students. They are remunerated for this tutoring, and the results show that the tutors' own achievements benefit from this experience. The fact of teaching, of explaining and putting knowledge into context for the younger students, forces them to structure their knowledge and ask questions which they might not have asked had they not been tutors. In New Caledonia, a teacher from the university organizes support on site and checks that the students are actually following the course remotely. The solution of tutoring from more advance students is quite common; this interaction may take place online or in person, the idea being that both parties will benefit from the exchange. In the project TIL[8], which is a distance master's course in gerontology, piloted by Marcel Spector, inspired by the ultrasound experiment from Senegal, the tutor is part of the concept; tutors are trained in all the universities participating in the project. The participants are enrolled in each of the participating universities (whichever they prefer), and the registration fee is $800, which helps to balance the budget and pay the tutors.

The experiment in Medicine teaching leads us to think that a tutoring "industry" could be established around certain free MOOCs. Indeed, in the first year of Medicine, in France, in numerous faculties, nearly all students rely on backroom tutoring sessions to help prepare for their competitive exams. In other words, they pay tutors on top of a course delivered in a traditional manner by the university. The same system could be transposed and used for MOOCs, provided the stakes are high enough and there is a demand for tutors which can be fulfilled.

All these experiences and considerations have convinced us that in the context of initial training (particularly during the first few years at university), the services of a tutor are practically indispensable. Another way of looking at the matter is to say that a MOOC, instead of being addressed to a massive number of registered students, is destined for a "normal" class who have a natural tutor: the professor! When a MOOC is used to teach small groups, in the form of a SPOC[9], it delivers excellent results. Armando Fox, professor at the University

8 Trans Innov Longévité – a distance-learning project in gerontology run by three French universities (http://www.til.cerimes.fr/index1/php). This project which is part of IDEFI initiative (*initiatives d'excellence en formations innovantes* – Innovative Initiatives for Educational Excellence) is experimenting a master degree teaching, on a distance basis, distributed between several universities, with tutors.

9 See section 1.3.

of Berkeley, who devised the acronym SPOC, stresses the fact that, if the students have taken the MOOC, then the dialog with the teacher will be much more fruitful, which enables the session to focus more on what has not been understood. Khosrow Ghadiri, from the University of San Jose, observed that the use of a *Udacity* course had led to a very high failure rate, whereas in an electronic course on *edX* in the form of a SPOC – i.e. using the flipped-classroom technique – 91% of students passed the course. However, like Cima, Ghadiri must admit that the transformation of typical classes into flipped classes is a labor-intensive task. The resources employed in these experiments were not used elsewhere; this has led to opposition at San José State University, and even stark opposition, an echo of which can be found in Steve Kolowich's article[10]. Hence, in university teaching, we feel that the tutored MOOC has a much brighter future than the non-tutored MOOC, and in conclusion, SPOCs or flipped classrooms seem to us the way to go, with all or parts of online courses being integrated into a "normal" course, commented on by a teacher and evaluated each week.

If a tutor or mentor is not available, in public usage or distance learning, it is necessary to count on the community – either the remote virtual community or the local community, at a *meetup* – to stimulate motivation and commentate on the course, and personal or professional influences will help participants to persevere and follow the course to completion. Certain MOOCs – particularly cMOOCs – make an effort to recreate a classroom atmosphere by obliging MOOCers to enroll in groups which share work and comments. If small active groups of followers of a given MOOC form, the model has every chance of working, but with a dropout rate that will, nevertheless, remain very high – higher than 50%.

Note, finally, that up until now, in our estimations of the cost of MOOCs – particularly in Chapter 2 – we have made the hypothesis that having a tutor is optional and is not included in the estimates.

10 On the polemic at San José, see Steve Kolowich, 2013: http://chronicle.com/article/A-Truce-Over-Technology/143229/ and http://chronicle.com/ article/Why-Professors-at-San-Jose/138941/.

4

Financing and Development of MOOCs

4.1. What benefits do MOOCs bring, and what profits can be made?

4.1.1. *In universities*

For a university which decides to replace its conventional teaching units with MOOCs, the financial return is not clear: a MOOC is more demanding in terms of workload than the corresponding conventional unit, except in the case of large cohorts and repetitive teaching, at least three consecutive years according to our estimations.

The use of MOOCs in the flipped-classroom methodology requires a huge amount of human resources – at least for the first round of the MOOC. Thus, a MOOC is only likely to break even if it is repeated multiple times and has a large number of participants. It is only undergraduate courses and a few bottleneck degrees which might be able to generate a return on investment because, in this latter case, MOOCs can prevent the need to open additional facilities. When the MOOC is free, and there is no primary intention to use it internally for mass teaching or a refresher course, it will either be financed philanthropically or by taking the money away from a budget line other than education (communication, international action, etc.). For a university, reintegrating students from a MOOC back into classic-format courses by putting them through a paying conventional final exam may be another way to recoup some of the costs of developing the MOOC.

We may envisage paying enrollments, as operated by *Udacity*. Selling off-the-shelf courses to less reputable universities, which thereby avoiding having to hire specialists from outside, may be the model employed by *Coursera*. However, it is not certain that local professors will be overly keen to become tutors on a course developed at Harvard or Stanford. Certain professors from San José have clearly expressed their opposition, and they will certainly not be the last to do so[1]. The sharing of a ready-made course for universities or organizations which do not have the means to develop their own is certainly the most realistic way forward today. Certain universities would construct MOOCs and make them available to their partners who do not have the same resources. The institutions making use of these courses would supplement them with local tutoring, which is much less costly and easier to organize than recruiting the professionals needed to write the course. It is necessary to put in place a system to compensate the universities which supply the courses, if they are provided for free.

4.1.2. *Continuing education*

Continuing education is now the favored domain of MOOCs, for various reasons which we have already mentioned: attractiveness of new technologies, greater flexibility than face-to-face teaching, and the possibility of attracting learners who are unable to be present or who are not of the typical age to attend school or university.

In continuing education, the problem for the universities is the attractiveness of what they have to offer, and its adequacy in relation to professional demands. MOOCs represent one viable way forward, but are not the solution to the problem of hunting for customers. Doctors, for whom continuing education is an obligation, did not wait for the emergence of MOOCs to take courses on conventional distance-learning management systems which, in their usage, are already very similar to many MOOCs. We have seen that in the cost of a MOOC, the initial investment, which is always relatively high, is

1 Why Professors at San José State won't use a Harvard professor's MOOC, Steve Kolowich, 2013, http://chronicle.com/article/Why-Professors-at-San-Jose/138941/.

between $50,000 and $200,000, not including "*operating expenditure*" (OPEX). In the OPEX, a distinction must be drawn between personnel costs for the university and the organization of recruitment of tutors, which is an additional expense. An experiment in France purporting to a distance-learning course in gerontology, the TIL[2] project, tends to show that if each participant pays a reasonable fee of around $800 subscription a year, this counterbalances the costs of operating the MOOC – i.e. to a large extent, the tutors' payment is handled. This sum to obtain an 8-credit professional qualification is realistic in a corporate context, but it is less easily envisageable for university students.

Returning to the subject of universities, the experiment of the Master of Science in Computer Science program at Georgia Tech, hosted by *Udacity*, demonstrates ([HOL 14], case 5) that even if the amount of enrollment fees required drops from $12,820 (in the first the course runs) to $4,212 in the third year, for 36 credits, the total balance is not offset for the university unless we are optimistic about the number of students enrolling. The same conclusion could be drawn for all experiments, to date, of transforming traditional courses into flipped classes using MOOCs. In addition, Sebastian Thrun, the founder of *Udacity*, has recently declared that MOOCs at university are not financially viable (see section 4.2).

Briefly, with regard to public institutions, in that higher education is highly subsidized, no-one in Europe actually envisages the possibility of a 100% financial return, except perhaps EPFL, who seek to attract new students who would pay substantial enrollment fees. In the United States, in that students pay for an increasingly high percentage of their education, the issue is still live, and it doubles as another issue: why should students pay an additional cost for a MOOC which is not included in a flipped-class framework – in other words, why pay for a course that is entirely online? The response is certainly negative: they will not pay! In light of the fact that, besides the cost of Teaching Assistant services, a MOOC costs around three times as much as does a face-to-face course – at least for its first use – MOOCs are destined to remain subsidized by the establishments in question.

2 Trans Innov Longévité – previously cited.

4.1.3. *Value of data*

The acquisition of personal data, or *big data,* is a relevant (and sensitive) subject in relation to the Web today. "*Learning analytics*" and "*data tracking*" are no exception. These terms cover the use of the dataset amassed from each visit by the participants to a MOOC and their path. The records of these visits are known as logs. The LMSs which host MOOCs obviously collect such logs and provide the results – which, in principle, should have been anonymized – to the creators of the MOOCs. They contain all relevant information about the MOOCers' behavior: login times and session durations, pages/documents consulted and the duration of those consults, exercises completed, most frequently-asked questions (FAQs) and all traces of interactions with the system. The data are enriched with anything which might contribute to an understanding of the students' behavior. There are some projects which go as far as recording the working conditions, the way in which the users' eyes move, their pattern of keystrokes, etc. These data can be exploited for commercial purposes or used to pedagogical ends. Yet the information collected may become highly intrusive. Any data collection must conform to the *FERPA requirements*. FERPA (Family Educational Rights and Privacy Act) prohibits the "*improper disclosure of personally identifiable information derived from education records*". As we can see, in principle, it is not acceptable to sell data other than statistics. *Coursera* recently announced officially that it would not sell data, which had (at one point) been envisaged in its financial model. It seems that *edX* has never envisaged selling data, but that it does provide raw, non-anonymized data to only one data coordinator at each partner institution ([HOL 14], p. 128). In any case, for American LMSs, selling data could only represent a very marginal source of income because of FERPA. In theory, they could hope to sell information likely to serve to build up learner profiles corresponding to the requirements of various employers and "head-hunters". This subject is a sensitive, ethically-tricky one, and specialists doubt the viability of this business model. It is one of the crucial points when choosing to use any for-profit LMS, in that the personal data become the property of these organizations and the participants are, *de facto*, obliged to submit those data without knowing what use will be made of them. In addition, it is worth mentioning that European universities are also subject to laws concerning the exportation of personal data beyond the European Union. Finally, it should be mentioned that the data generated by the various LMSs are not interoperable, but that talks have begun on this issue between *Coursera*, *edX* and *Udacity*.

For universities which make use of MOOCs, these data help to provide students with an additional service: the exams provide validation of their knowledge, and their activity profiles also help to measure their skills. We can envisage that in the future these profiles will become more important than the exams alone. What is also hugely important is the possibility of identifying promising learners and attracting them to come to the university which posted the course online. Stanford and MIT offer grants to people who have done exceptionally well on their MOOCs. This "*brain-drain*" system is obviously a real danger for universities of lesser repute. In the context of lifelong learning, the creation of a portfolio of credentials from the existing logs is a necessity, and it could come to represent an alternative to university or college credits. The nascent technology of "badges" could provide the solution[3].

These data also represent valuable elements for researchers in educational sciences. They could be used to help create "smart" LMSs, capable of providing learning paths that are personalized on the basis of a set of criteria collected previously during the course. An early LMS for MOOCs, founded on this principle, has been announced in Japan, and major projects are being funded at this moment. In Europe, on this topic, we can cite POEMs (*Personalised Open Education for the Masses*)[4] – a project spearheaded by the University of Strasbourg. Although we are not exactly starting from zero – there are already a number of works in this domain of "smart" tracking of learners (see [BRU 97, BAR 07]), it will still be many years before we are able to implement truly intelligent mechanisms, but the area is a promising one. In the immediate future, the most valuable use of the data collected is analysis by the teachers on the MOOC to improve their course for the next cohort. In fact,

3 For example, see http://www.openbadges.org/.

4 http://cnsc.unistra.fr/cncs/index.php/POEMS_(Personalised_Open_ Education_for_the_ Masses).

it must be noted that we are still a long way from being able to offer personalized education which adapts to each individual student in real time. It is a fertile area for research, but there is still a long way to go. Put simply, "it is apparent that while the potential for MOOCs to contribute significantly to the development of personalized learning is high, the reality is far from being achieved. A great deal of coordination and collaboration among researchers, instructional designers, and programmers will be necessary to result in meaningful improvements to teaching and learning" ([HOL 14], p. 133).

In order for the data exploitation system to become widely accepted, it is also necessary to deal with legal and ethical questions: who owns the data? What guarantees are given to the students regarding their anonymity? And so on. This is only one of the aspects of the issues raised, today, by the acquisition of personal data. Students are sensitive about this issue: some have complained to EPFL for having forced them to supply their data to *Coursera*, without knowing exactly what was to be done with them. When it was pointed out that they frequently openly provide such data on *Facebook*, they quite rightly responded that in the case of Facebook, they provided the data as a conscious choice – deliberately and personally.

4.2. Financing of MOOCs

Apart from the occasional exception, all the organizations which professionally develop MOOCs have chosen a private business structure. They use private capital, possibly supplemented by funds from the universities and foundations. By mid-2013, *Coursera*, which is a commercial enterprise, had raised $85 million[5] from diverse venture-capital structures or parties interested in an innovative area, such as the World Bank, having started with $16 million in 2012, which was provided by Kleiner Perkins Caufield & Byers. Similarly, *Udacity*, founded by Sebastian Thrun[6] with David Stavens and Mike

5 http://www.marketwired.com/press-release/coursera-secures-43m-funding-from-gsv-capital-ifc-laureate-education-inc-learn-capital-nasdaq-gsvc-1809772.htm.

6 Article by Max Chafkin, Udacity's Sebastian Thrun, Godfather of free online education, changes courses, http:// www.fastcompany.com/3021473/ udacity-sebastian-thrun-uphill-climb.

Sokolsky, started in 2012 with $15 million from Charles River Ventures, and a year later, received a further $15-million injection from Andreessen Horowitz.

Coursera relies, for its business, on partner universities which give it their courses to host. These universities receive the hosting services for free, but depending on the contract, pay a certain percentage of the revenue generated by the use of the MOOC and the certification. In addition, *Coursera* keeps all proceeds from the sale of auxiliary products relating to the exploitation of the data. *Udacity* also relies on partners, but produces its own courses in its studio. Its relationship with the universities, therefore, is much more tenuous, to the point that, at the end of 2013, Sebastian Thrun declared that funding of the company by the provision of services for higher education was no longer working, and that *Udacity* was going to turn to the provision of training for businesses[7].

The approaches of *Coursera* and *Udacity* are different. *Udacity* creates content whereas *Coursera* forms partnerships with known universities, with the objective of providing the best and most popular courses.

The third significant LMS is *edX*; once again, it is an American platform launched by MIT and Harvard. The launch of *edX* benefited from MIT's experience in the area of distance learning, with its platform *OpenCourseWare*; *edX* chose to go down a non-commercial route, although it takes 50% of revenue generated by the MOOC, with a minimum of several thousand dollars. A private organization, it was set up as a foundation, with $60 million funding from Harvard, MIT and the Bill and Melinda Gates Foundation.

The aim of the *Khan Academy*, founded in 2006, is to "reinvent education", because its founder, Salman Khan, had seen the difficulties children had in learning mathematics in class, and noted that they had more success when learning on the computer with

7 Article by J.K. Waters: "*Breaking the MOOC model*", Campus technology, January 2014, http://online.qmags.com/CPT0114?pg=7&mode=1#pg18& mode1.

interactive games. Salman Khan's main ideas can be found in his book: "*The One World Schoolhouse*" [KHA 12]. The *Khan Academy*, unlike *Coursera*, is a not-for-profit organization like *edX* (see Figure 4.2). It has received support from numerous foundations[8], including the Bill and Melinda Gates Foundation, totaling over $20 million, and from Eric Schmidt, the chairman of Google, totaling $17 million, via his foundation and Google's shareholders. The main target of the *Khan Academy* is late-primary and secondary-school education, supplemented by the showing of short, highly-instructive videos. The *Khan Academy* provides services in sixty languages, and over 300 million people have viewed one of the 6,000 available videos. Having a course in video format obviously allows the learner to watch the lectures as many times as he or she wishes, until he or she understands fully. The use of video does not preclude the role of a normal teacher: the philosophy is one of "*blended learning*". However, unlike a teacher, a video will never get tired of repeating itself!

Moreover, certain LMSs, using the same idea as Internet search engines, believe they can survive on the money generated by advertising. This is the view of Mike Feerick, founder of *ALISON* (2007), who devotes his Website to open, free education in poor countries; his published figures suggest a following of two million learners in these countries, thus rivalling the *Khan Academy*.

Another model is championed by Ben Nelson – the founder of *Snapfish* – who proposes to use online courses without depriving the students of the advantages of attending a campus. He raised $25 million in funding to set up the company *MINERVA*. The concept is of a university where students pursue courses online, but from different campuses all over the world, which helps the students discover the world and socialize, because the whole class of students moves around, but still have remote access to the teacher. Costs involved run to about $30,000 a year for teaching and accommodation.

---

8 See www.insidephilanthropy.com/home/2014/6/26/the-funders-pouring-money-into-the-Khan-Academy.html.

coursera	KHANACADEMY	U	edX
Coursera is a for-profit organization set up by two professors from Stanford University (Andrew Ng and Daphne Koller). Coursera provides a content platform and establishes partnerships with renowned universities, which take care of the organization of the courses and provision of the content.	Established in 2006 by Salman Khan, the Khan Academy is a pioneer of the MOOC movement. With the aim of changing the face of education, the Khan Academy offers quality courses accessible, for free, to most people.	Udacity is a for-profit organization founded by another Stanford professor: Sebastian Thrun. Unlike Coursera, Udacity only establishes partnerships with individual professors rather than with universities. Thus, the teachers post the content online directly.	A not-for-profit public consortium, edX was created by Harvard and MIT. Other universities such as Berkeley have joined the consortium, and nine more are expected to join in the coming months. Thus, the courses delivered were developed only at those universities which belong to edX.

Figure 4.1. *Main actors in the world of MOOCs*

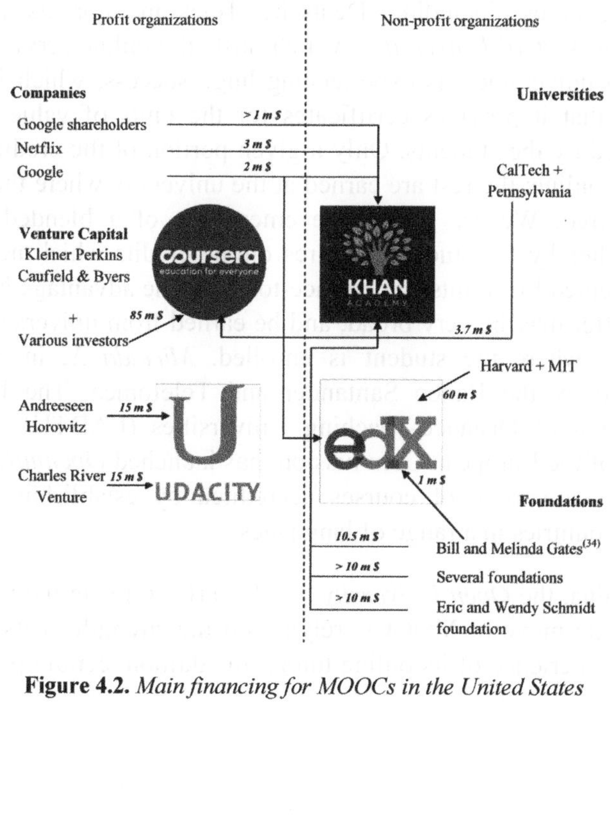

Figure 4.2. *Main financing for MOOCs in the United States*

One of the major turning points in the "MOOC Revolution" occurred in June 2013, when *edX* released the source code for its platform. The release of the *edX* code, under the title *OpenedX*, was seen as a true revolution, because it enabled many more platforms to be developed at a low cost. Thereafter, anyone could create content and share it with the rest of the world. On 10 September 2013, Google announced that it was joining *edX* to help develop the *OpenedX* portal.

In Europe, the various countries are organizing, pending a hypothetical wide-ranging European initiative. In Great Britain, *FutureLearn* includes over 20 universities (23, to be exact, at the start of 2014), alongside the British Library, under the auspices of the *Open University*, and has received \$20 million in private funds. *FutureLearn* is opening up its LMS and expertise to the outside world; it has just concluded an agreement with the South Korean university Yonsei. *Iversity*, in Germany, received over €1 million from BFB Frühphasenfonds Brandenburg (EU 75% and Brandenburg 25%) and BMP's media investors in July 2011, followed by venture capital from several sources, including Deutsche Telekom. For its part, the "*Bavarian Virtual University*", which hosts the online services of the Bavarian universities, is experiencing huge success, which is due to the fact that it provides certificates for the units of value (credits) completed by the students. Only a given portion of the credits can be obtained online; the rest are earned at the university where the student is registered. We are seeing the emergence of a blended-learning model whereby the student acquires online credits which need to be supplemented by credits earned face-to-face. The advantage is that the online offer may be very broad, and be earned from universities other than that where the student is enrolled. *Miriada X*, in Spain, is supported by the Banco Santander and Telefónica. The European Association of Distance-Teaching Universities (EADTU), with the support of the European Commission, has launched *OpenupEd*, which advertises a variety of courses accredited by establishments from various countries in a range of languages.

In China, the *Open University of China* (OUC) is in the process of making the move to MOOCs, relying on the strength of its network and the experience of its online tutors. In addition, certain prestigious universities under the guidance of Tsinghua have come together to form a consortium, to create and operate the Chinese portal, *XueTangX*, which is based on *OpenedX* and was launched in October 2013. This consortium includes or has included the Universities of Nanjing and Shanghai Jiao Tong; the latter has now launched CNMOOC. Peking University, with the encouragement of a pioneer of MOOCs, Professor Xiaoming Li, has chosen *Coursera* to host its MOOCs. Similarly, in Australia, *Open Universities Australia* runs the portal *Open2Study*. Most of these initiatives, which are based on previous expertise gained in online teaching, deliver courses for free and intend to start awarding ECTS credits.

All these schemes imitate the American model set by *Coursera* and *edX*, establishing close relationships with the universities.

Numerous start-up companies are attempting to find a place in the online teaching market to take advantage of the current desire for MOOCs. For example, *Learning Shelter* is beginning to adopt a stance in relation to private online courses, "tutored" in the sense in which we explained it in section 3.4 – i.e. with a "mentor", to use the vocabulary adopted by the company. We can see that similar types of private initiatives are beginning to increase in number.

In the world of French-speaking university education, a number of prestigious establishments (ENS Ulm, ENS Lyon, Polytechnique, Catholic University of Leuven, *Ecole Polytechnique de Montréal* and EPFL) have recently launched the portal *OCEAN*, which is designed for MOOCs given only in French. As one would expect from such prestigious institutions as these, quality control is carried out by an editorial committee, with the portal functioning like an academic journal. The target audience for *OCEAN* is the whole of the French-speaking world.

In France, the system *FUN* (*France Université Numérique*) was launched by the Ministry for Research and Higher Education on 2 October 2013. Based on the model of *edX*, *FUN* is organized in the form of an academic cooperative foundation. In the view of certain admirers of *OCEAN*, it would be desirable for *FUN* to turn more toward the international scene, with a particular emphasis on

French-speaking countries[9]. *FUN* has around 300,000 registered students, according to the Ministry, and more than 25 MOOCs have been conducted between January 2014 and the summer of the same year; more than 70 before the end of the year. In terms of the international scene, we can see stirrings of interest in Africa (7% of students).

FUN has opted for a tripartite operational model similar to that used by *Coursera* and *edX*: the development of a course results from the signing of an agreement between the establishment to which the teacher belongs, the teacher, and the foundation. Hence, it is not possible for an isolated individual to post their course on the system. The learning management system chosen – namely *OpendedX* – is being adapted for the French audience. This tripartite mechanism could possibly be demolished in the near future: *edX* and *Google* have recently signed a cooperation agreement leading, amongst other things, to the creation of an LMS *mooc.org* on which absolutely anybody can start offering a course of their choice. Free provision of courses as happens at the *Khan Academy* could lead to questions being asked, in the future, about the role of the universities as guardians of quality.

In conclusion, at present, there is no viable economic model to sustain the development of MOOCs in a university context. For example, the 2013 revenues for *Coursera*, based on the sale of verified certificates, total only $1 million[10]. Consequently, either MOOCs must attract paying audiences from a broader base than university or college students, expanding to cater to school-age children and offer support courses to compensate for the inadequacies of school education (a little like the *Khan Academy* does), or they must become essential elements in lifelong learning in a business environment. Otherwise they will simply become objects of prestige or subsidized research, or indeed, the unprofitable trailblazers of an educational revolution, as we shall discuss in the next chapter.

9 See the adventures of "Pedagotix": https://plus.google.com/106199448686907260931/posts.

10 See https//gigaom.com/2013/09/12/coursera-hits-1m-in-revenue-through-verified-certificates.

5

MOOCs and Higher Education

MOOCs arouse significant passions in the field of education. Is the phenomenon a revolution, as certain people claim? If so, is it an educational revolution or an institutional revolution, with the demise of certain higher education institutions? Will MOOCs destroy academia? [VAR 12][1]. For his part, the founder of *Udacity*, Sebastian Thrun, in a very well-known article published in *Wired* in 2012[2], predicted that most American universities would close within ten years, although it must be noted that his opinion has changed since then (see section 4.2). Finally, we should cite Nathan Harden's article in The American Interest, 2012 [HAR 12], whose title is revealing: "The End of the University as we Know it[3]", and begins with these words: "*In fifty years, if not much sooner, half of the roughly 4,500 colleges and universities now operating in the United States will have ceased to exist. The technology driving this change is already at work, and nothing can stop it. The future looks like this: access to college-level education will be free for everyone; the residential college campus will become largely obsolete; tens of thousands of professors will lose their jobs; the bachelor's degree will become increasingly*

1 M.Y. Vardi, 2012, Communications of the ACM, Vol. 55, No. 11, Page 5, http://cacm.acm.org/magazines/2012/11/156587-will-moocs-destroy-academia/fulltext.

2 http://www.wired.com/2012/03/ff_aiclass/all/.

3 http://www.the-american-interest.com/articles/2012/12/11/the-end-of-the-university-as-we-know-it/.

irrelevant; and ten years from now Harvard will enroll ten million students."

5.1. MOOCs and universities

In order to estimate the impact that MOOCs have on universities' policies and reflect on their future relations, it is, at the very least, necessary to gain a clear understanding of what exactly constitutes a university.

5.1.1. *What is a university?*

At the root of it, a university is a community of teachers and students which has gained autonomy from the religious and temporal authorities to devote itself to knowledge and learning to think: creation of new knowledge, research and teaching of the "truth", critical examination of all past knowledge or knowledge under construction; in a distorted but essential way, it is also the place where teachers gain their degrees – i.e. essentially the right to teach but particularly to enjoy certain privileges.

Nowadays, in principle, it remains an institution which is autonomous (dependent on local circumstances) from the religious and temporal powers, pursuing the same original goals as (recapped above), and which almost always exclusively leads to certain career paths, including teaching, law and medicine, and is in competition with all sorts of training institutions specializing in other areas.

5.1.2. *Who is the target market for a university?*

The idea of a community of teachers and students, which held a great deal of sway originally, has now been dethroned somewhat by that of a community of teachers. However, owing to the significant presence of former students (*alumni*) and their role in the governance of the universities, the universities in the English-speaking world have maintained something of the alliance between teachers and students. Previously, the close connection between teachers and students was an unavoidable part of education: students would become graduates and then gain their doctorates, in the spirit of close companionship with one or more teachers. Obviously, the number of students involved has meant the companionship in higher education has largely dissolved, at least at undergraduate and masters' level, but the idea holds true at the level of doctoral studies.

Given that, after all, universities are made for students, let us examine exactly what it is that we understand by "student". Is a student, first and foremost, someone seeking a degree – a certificate qualifying him/her for employment and/or social position – or someone who is attracted by knowledge and learning? Is a student attempting, by way of research and the company of wise people and teachers, to learn to think, to acquire their own truth, intellectual independence, and the critical mind which will make them a true citizen? In fact, it is a little of all of these things, mixed in varying proportions in each student.

Yet realistically, it must be noted that above all, what the vast majority of students are looking for is employability – a certificate which holds value in the jobs market. With this goal in mind, the way in which it is achieved is of little importance – people may even commit fraud or obtain a pseudo-diploma from certain institutions with an aggressive "marketing" strategy based on employability; the result counts more than the content. However, in order to obtain that result – i.e. a lucrative job – the qualification in question needs to be relatively rare. Hence, students (or rather, their families) look for qualifications which are not too easy to obtain – or, even better, a qualification from a school or university which is selective even from the very earliest moments of studies; this selectiveness affords a considerable advantage to the children of culturally fortunate families. The "customers" for higher education are at least as much the families as the students themselves, and the families favor selectiveness; in other words, they are not spontaneously predisposed to openness!

In summary, there are few students who originally enroll at university in order to acquire intellectual independence, a critical understanding of the state of the world, with a view to creating new knowledge or seeking out the company of great minds – although, ultimately, they get something out of the experience in other than the certificate they initially came to get. Obviously, these issues are less and less present as we get closer to doctoral level.

5.1.3. *Which universities?*

The result of the above pressures is that universities are being led to specialize increasingly, depending on their target audience. A minority of universities rally brilliant students who, above all – above their diplomas, even – seek to integrate "the international community of knowledge" and gain plaudits for their research. A MOOC is not the companionship-based education which is so typical at doctoral level; in fact it is the polar opposite of such an education, because the teacher who developed the course is a long way away from the students, even if they do answer e-mails sent to them. Consequently, primarily-research-oriented universities occupy an economic niche, which shelters them from competition from MOOCs in terms of their teaching, although they may make use of MOOCs in their teaching programs, as we shall see later on. On the other hand, for prestigious universities, the launching of MOOCs designed for external audiences across the globe is a goal, because it safeguards and even strengthens their reputation and prestige if the MOOC becomes a "must". Furthermore, launching a successful MOOC helps them to attract students from all over the world and improve their chances of detecting the brilliant doctorates of the future.

It is other higher education institutions which cater to the demand for qualifications, and respond to the need to belong to a prestigious and powerful community of alumni. In certain cases at well-known universities, the community aspect is prevalent; in others, it is the professional aspect and the value of the professional qualification which count, in courses such as engineering, medicine, law, agronomy, etc. The quest to belong to a community is not affected by MOOCs, rather, it is courses which are largely (or partly) aimed at instilling vocational skills, of lesser prestige (i.e. which have lower entry requirements), which are most threatened by competition from MOOCs. Of course, this observation, which also holds true for the various non-research higher education institutions, be they public or private, can be extended to universities where the intensity of research is low. It is from this perspective that MOOCs are sometimes seen as a threat for universities. In the United States, nearly all PhDs are awarded by about 400 universities out of the 4,500 existing higher education establishments. Why pay to enroll at any of the other 4,100 establishments when it is possible, from one's own home, to gain a degree from Harvard, by having taken a course given by a prestigious professor?

5.1.4. *MOOCs in universities and the "educational revolution"*

Is the wave of MOOCs going to wash traditional teaching away? Some people think so, and many hope so! It is unsurprising that one of the founders of *Coursera* is Daphne Koller, who was a proponent of the "flipped classroom" experiments at Stanford.

Note, to begin with, that master-to-pupil teaching is the only human activity which, should an Ancient Greek be restored to life today, he would find greatly similar to how it was in Plato's time. He would recognize the small group of students, the lectern, and the teacher discoursing at the front; only the content would seem different to him. For this reason, many people speak of their wish for a "modernization" of education and a digital "revolution".

How can MOOCs aid in this modernization? The primary argument states, simply, that MOOCs replaces teacher-centered (*ex-cathedra*) lessons, thereby freeing both the students and the teachers for exercises, personalized supervision and "coaching". Put differently, students follow the MOOC and hence gain a certain amount of "teacher time", for an in-depth dialog with the supervisors (teachers or tutors). As we saw earlier, the expression "flipped teaching" is used to describe this situation. Why "flipped"? Because it is the learner who becomes "master of the dialog" after having taken the MOOC. J. Bergmann and A. Sams, the inventors of the "*flipped-classroom*" approach, summarize the main advantages and disadvantages to flipped pedagogy on the Website "*The Daily Riff*"[4]:

– flipped pedagogy offers a way of increasing interaction between the teacher and the learner, and increasing learner involvement;

– the teacher is not an omniscient figure talking down from on high, but rather becomes a "guide", walking beside the student;

– the approach offers a way of personalizing the teaching and keeping a permanent record thereof, and hence overcomes the time constraint resulting from having the same class for everyone in the same place.

However, in flipped classrooms, students are not simply placed in front of a screen to replace the teacher. Nor is a flipped course an unstructured experience where the student is isolated[5]. *Flipped teaching, in the minds of its inventors, remains a course of teaching, with professors*. Fox [FOX 13] also clearly states that it is a true educational experience with additional resources: "*supplementing the classroom experience with small private online courses*". Thus, whilst the two movements (flipped pedagogy and MOOCs) are used in conjunction with one another, they are not the same thing. However, they have in common the idea of a digital class which the student can (and must) watch, before interaction with the teacher in the case of flipped teaching, and before the exercises and discussion in the case of the MOOC. We can consider a tutored MOOC to be a compromise between the two approaches (see section 3.4).

There is, of course, a utopian aspect in this reinvention of teaching, because obviously, the lambda student would likely be no more active watching a MOOC, lying on the couch eating pizza, than sitting in a lecture theater, sending text messages under the desk. However, with motivated students, in small groups, given the necessary resources in terms of teachers and tutors, it is likely that this type of teaching will be able to help a large number of students. In other words, at

4 http://www.thedailyriff.com/articles/how-the-flipped-classroom-is-radically-transforming-learning-536.php.

5 Also see https://plus.google.com/s/lebrunremy.be.

universities, the future of MOOCs lies partly in SPOCs and the various forms of flipped teaching. Hence, little by little, MOOCs are undoubtedly going to change the role of the teacher who, having taught *ex-cathedra* classes, has the opportunity to once again become an involved tutor, attentive to the student's progression.

Certain universities, such as EPFL or Lille 1, have conducted experiments in this area, in an attempt to find an alternative to the formal lectures of the first years of university. Let us emphasize this use of MOOCs as substitutes or chosen alternatives to lecture-theater-based classes. As noted above, undergraduate students are less and less able, these days, to concentrate on an *ex-cathedra* class: they already have one eye, or both, on their mobiles or tablets. Thus, it is perfectly conceivable for all mass classes to be given in MOOC format, to be watched at the student's convenience, with the teacher's "contact time" being reserved for applied work classes. This is a prospect which, to our minds, is both desirable and unavoidable.

In the same vein, another experience was launched at University of Pennsylvania, the program SAIL (Structured, Active, In-class Learning program) is intended to "support faculty in reimagining classes to emphasize the active engagement of students in class through structured works, guided by the instructor". A part of the material provided to the students is online and "the instructors often ask students to master some content before coming to class".

In other words, as observed in section 3.4, we believe that in initial university teaching, the future lies with tutored MOOCs: i.e. a mixture of online classes to be followed in students' own time and face-to-face group classes. We have also seen that the experiments in flipped teaching mainly show an improvement in students' attainment – particularly for those students who are less strong to begin with. Ultimately, there is only one major drawback to flipped teaching: it costs between 3 and 4 times as much as normal teaching. Why is this? Because it is necessary to design and create the online classes, whether we actually call them a MOOC or not; it is necessary to design and create the weekly assessments; to train a large number of teaching assistants or tutors; and open up classrooms to accommodate small groups of learners in Face-to-Face Interactive Complementary Classes (FICCs).

On the other hand, flipped teaching undoubtedly helps to have more students with a fuller understanding, and represents one potential solution for bottleneck courses. We can quote the view of Fox (in [HOL 14]): "*The biggest benefit of the SPOC in our setting is that we've been able to multiply by almost a factor five the number of students who can take our class... Historically we were limited by the number of assignments we could grade and the number of TAs we could hire. Now the TA ratio hasn't changed but the TAs are spending their time quite differently. They're not grading assignments and exams because we have automation to do a lot of that. They're not rehashing what was said in the lecture because students can go watch that stuff online if they miss a lecture, or if they didn't get it in the first time around. They're not creating finger exercises because we've included those along with the lectures; it's the same as the peer learning questions that we use. We put those online as well so students can review from them. The TAs can focus on higher leverage activities.*" This quote is a little long, but it clearly illustrates how, in a somewhat idealistic world, the introduction of flipped teaching changes the role of the teachers and helps improve the quality of the teaching. It is far less easy to say whether the attendant increase in the number of students will actually balance out the costs of developing a SPOC.

Beyond offering a classic course in the form of a MOOC, we can envisage using MOOCs for less conventional purposes, such as refresher courses; the acquisition of prerequisites before a course and preparation of the students to follow that course; the revision of modules which the student has already taken in order to help them when re-sitting an exam; the support of students who are ill or have commitments to events such as training sessions or away fixtures for athletes, for example. Thus, EDHEC has created a 100% online option for high-level athletes. We can see that there are numerous possible gainful uses of MOOCs for students enrolled at universities.

5.1.5. *The end for universities?*

Certain apocalyptic descriptions, examples of which are given in the introduction to this chapter, view the upsurge in the use of MOOCs as marking the end for universities. A French creator of a start-up in the digital domain, Gilles Babinet, predicts a revolution identical to the printing revolution: "*Just like in the Middle Ages, Gutenberg emptied the abbeys. Tomorrow, MOOCs will empty the universities*[6]". All these bleak "projections" are reminiscent of the predictions made in 1956 about the "Artificial Intelligence Revolution"; Herbert Simon's followers, and Simon himself, were certainly not wrong – computers are not fated to only perform calculations; they were also right in predicting that machines would soon be as intelligent as humans and would proliferate in all domains of life, except that, whilst ICT has indeed taken over our daily lives and makes possible huge numbers of things that would have been unimaginable 50 years ago, "the revolution has taken 60 years, and it is not over yet". However, when we think in terms of revolution, we tend to think of events occurring within a relatively short time-period. Distance learning, though, as indicated in Chapter 1, has long been a reality, with materials being sent by post; televised education has existed for 50 years. At this juncture, the primary author of this book would like to share a personal recollection: as a young math teacher in the experimental Henri Martin School in Saint-Quentin, Aisne, in 1966, I recorded my first televised classes, intended for sixth-graders. It worked well: the pupils learned a great deal in this way, but it was expensive to do, and required a massive investment of time and energy in order to work. The system could not be "upscaled", to use a term from IT; in other words, as soon as we tried to expand the system by moving the teacher/designer out of the teaching process to address many classrooms in parallel, the results were no longer as expected. Internal television circuits, as pedagogical tools, went down the drain a long time ago.

6 Original French: "*Gutenberg a vidé les abbayes au Moyen Age comme les MOOC videront les universités demain*". Le Nouvel Economiste, no. 1687, November 2013, "La déferlante des MOOC".

One of the arguments advanced by those who feel that MOOCs spell "the end of universities" is the financial argument: why would people pay for courses that they can take for free via a MOOC? On the one hand, it is undeniable that university – particularly in America – is extremely expensive: increasingly so. Government funding per student fell by 27% between 2007 and 2012, while the average tuition fees, adjusted for inflation, rose by 20%. On the other hand, MOOCs are free. Students should be able to "do the math" quite easily. However, it appears that this overpowering financial argument does not work, because in order for it to be justified from an accounting point of view, it is necessary to integrate the gains envisaged throughout a whole career. From that standpoint, the qualification gained and the relationships that can be forged at university remain a better investment. At least, it seems, this is the thinking of young people in countries where there is a plentiful supply of higher education.

On another point, as we have already observed, students between 18 and 25 years old go to university not only in search of knowledge and/or a certificate, but also in search of social growth, which a MOOC simply cannot replicate, even with its network of students. Thus, we do not believe that the days of universities are numbered. On the other hand, a transformation of the typical theater-based lecture[7] into an online course, within a greater or lesser period of time, is likely. In the fullness of time, this should drive down the cost of teaching in the early years of university, because repeatedly using a MOOC is cheaper than employing teachers over the same length of time. At present, the fees paid by undergraduate students go to support research which is of no benefit to those students; with MOOCs, students could pay a lower and fairer price.

In fact, "technology addicts" always make the same mistake: they forget that in order to learn, people need to know "the who and the why". Putting an individual in front of a screen has never answered these two fundamental questions, whereas presenting the student with a teacher (or, failing that, a tutor) partially answers the question: there

7 For example, see the experiment at UPMC: http://wiki.upmc.fr/x/4ICP.

is a living response. Even if the student is not learning for the sake of the teacher, all parents know that a child or teenager who does not like his/her teacher generally does not get good grades. Yet it has been clearly stated in writing by the theorists of flipped pedagogy: there is more to flipped teaching than simply seating the students in front of a screen and "leaving them to it". Nevertheless, for some people within the ranks of authority, this strategy would be perfectly acceptable, as it would save money on teachers. These people would like to see a MOOC revolution. Let us say it again, unequivocally: in early education, the future of MOOCs lies in tutored MOOCs for those who are unable to be physically present to take the class, and SPOCs for those who are at the universities. Remember that 72% of students taking the MOOCs run by Harvard or MIT live outside of the United States ([HOL 14], p. 57).

For all these reasons, it is likely to be a long road before higher education institutions are all forced to close because of lack of students. Nevertheless, certain teachers take this threat very seriously, to the point of taking their classes down from *Coursera*, as Mitchell Duneier, professor of sociology at Princeton, recently did[8]. In fact, those who are moved to write: "*MOOCs are one of the most powerful tools in the massive liquidation, which is taking place under our very noses, of what used to be called 'knowledge', which universities were supposed to transmit and produce. MOOCs resemble university courses as we know them in much the same way as Canada Dry resembles alcohol, but they are weapons of mass destruction which threaten knowledge and the university*[9]", have simply not taken the time to look at who studies on MOOCs and what their true added value is. Typical university students do not follow MOOCs, or at least

8 http://chronicle.com/article/A-MOOC-Star-Defects-at-Least/141331/.

9 Original French: "*Les MOOC… sont l'un des dispositifs de pointe dans la vaste liquidation, qui se déroule sous nos yeux, de ce qu'on avait coutume d'appeler "savoir" et qu'étaient supposées transférer et produire les universités. Comme le Canada Dry ressemble à de l'alcool, les MOOC ressemblent à des cours universitaires tels que nous les connaissons, mais ce sont des armes de destruction massives du savoir et de l'université* ". Pascal Engel in "Qualité de la Science Française", http://www.qsf.fr/ 2013/05/24/les-moocs-cours-massifs-ou-armes-de-destruction-massive.

not of their own volition. First and foremost, MOOCs are a tool for continuing education: ideally for everyone, but in fact, in the Western world, for those who already have a good education or a strong motivation or both. It is absolutely untrue, though, to say that MOOCs destroy knowledge: many MOOCs convey fascinating content, which is much better than that which is dispensed by the professors in many institutions, including universities. Obviously, though, in order to find out whether a MOOC is worthy, whether it is selling true or false science, one has to have taken the course and already have familiarity with the domain.

Another thing which lets down declarations similar to the one above is the absolute blindness to the situation on three quarters of Earth's landmass: i.e. all those countries where the provision of higher education is greatly insufficient. Would the detractors of MOOCs go so far as to give grants to the millions of students in Africa, Asia and Latin America, in whose countries there are few or no opportunities for higher education, so they can come and attend the classes of brilliant professors in rich countries, "*in the flesh*"? This would be in keeping with the logic of their positions, although perhaps they would prefer to finance the establishment of universities in those foreign countries.

Let us make the point, once again, that in countries which have a sufficient number of universities, MOOCs do not stand in the way of university education relating to research and knowledge creation; they are competitors for courses which dispense well-established, standard knowledge at a relatively low level, and which do not bring with them any significant degree of social recognition.

5.2. MOOCs and lifelong learning

In Chapter 3, we touched on this issue, noting that the most obvious potential target audience for MOOCs is a group who cannot conform to the constraints of time and place imposed by a conventional course imparted by a professor at a given time and place – in other words, all of the audience for lifelong learning. In addition to the aforementioned constraints, we also need to consider money constraints, because many MOOCs are likely to remain free, at least to enroll, and the certification will be relatively inexpensive.

In order to become widely accepted, this vision of MOOCs as vehicles for continuing education needs to be shared by businesses which, either internally or with content produced by outside contractors, would invite their employees to take MOOCs. The businesses, by paying for their employees' enrollment, would ensure that the providers of the MOOCs recoup their costs. Clearly, this is not unconnected to the certification: the credits obtained must be recognized by the agencies in charge of "government-mandated continuing education for professionals". The set of training courses taken would form a portfolio of credentials, which would be recognized in the same way as a college degree. Without this type of recognition of skills, the use of MOOCs in the world of business will remain restricted, but it is not beyond the bounds of possibility that certain countries such as the USA will turn to this tactic.

5.2.1. *At present, which are the largest groups of MOOC users?*

On this point, all reports are in agreement: at present, the majority of people enrolling on MOOCs are in search of continuing education. University students always form a small minority of spontaneous enrollments on a MOOC – rarely more than 15%. The University of Edinburgh observes the same thing in relation to its MOOCs on *Coursera*: they are followed by only 14.8% of students[10]. A normal student has very little motivation to take any courses other than those suggested by the teachers; indeed, sometimes, student are actually put off by the unspoken principle that anything that is not home-grown can only be bad! NIH (*not invented here*) is a very prevalent prejudice in teachers, and those who feel unable to recommend a book by an academic outside the university will, *a fortiori*, be very unlikely to recommend taking a MOOC! The other reason, as expressed by the philosophy professors at San José State University (see the end of section 3.4) is that professors have no desire to become the glorified teaching assistants of professors from other universities – either

10 See Lucile Quillet: http://etudiant.lefigaro.fr/les-news/actu/detail/article/cours-en-ligne-moins-d-un-participant-sur-cinq-est-etudiant-2672/.

because the latter are more famous, or (particularly galling) because they are simply brighter!

Remember that, from the very earliest days of MOOCs, the target audience has always been "everybody" – not just students. Thus, Sebastian Thrun's course on AI was taken by a considerable number of non-students, some of whom obtained outstanding results. In short, we can state that less than 15% of students enrolled on an undergraduate course (i.e. the first four or five years of university) will be tempted to enroll on courses – be they MOOCs or otherwise – which are not effusively recommended by their teachers – or, more simply, which are not part of their exams, as pointed out by Mathieu Cisel in his aforementioned blog: "*apprendre pour apprendre n'est pas valorisé*" (learning for learning's sake is not valued [in the exams]). On the other hand, if the MOOCs are part of the curriculum and earn credits, as is the case at MIT, the students do take them (50% of students at MIT have already taken a MOOC). Looking only at MOOCs which are not included in a university course, initial indications about the backgrounds of those who enroll show that the average age of the MOOCers is higher than the average age of university students (80% of enrolled people are aged over 25) and their level of study tends to be much higher than a bachelor's degree (80% of MOOCers are white-collar workers or executives with Master's degrees). *Coursera* reports that 83% of people taking their courses have already had higher education. All this suggests that people will consider willingly taking MOOCs from the age of 26-27 onwards!

After finishing their studies, people tend to come around once again to the idea of "learning something new". Owen Youngman[11] has already found, upon inquiry, that 90% of people who had obtained the certification from his MOOC already had a university degree. Those same people indicated that they feel themselves to be "more intelligent, better educated and better informed". It is important to note that the reasons given by MOOCers for pursuing a MOOC to completion tend to hinge around two arguments: 1) the prospect of

11 Jean-Sébastien Dubé in: http://www.ssfudes.com/veille/leveilleur/17513/ a-quoi-sert-lattestation-dun-mooc-des-etudiants-repondent/.

obtaining the certificate for successful completion of the course is an incentive to make an effort and a motivation to pursue it to the very end; 2) it is an achievement to put on their CV, which demonstrates their interest in a particular subject and their capacity to invest in that interest. It is the latter argument which would be put forward to a potential recruiter. This is a general observation which should be borne in mind: the majority of people taking MOOCs already have a university degree. In other words, MOOCs are used to supplement people's higher education – at least in countries where a majority of the population of university age has the possibility of accessing such education. Christiensen *et al.* [CHR 13] indicate that 79% of MOOCers at the University of Pennsylvania have a bachelor's degree and are over the age of 26. As a symptomatic illustration of this phenomenon, note that the MOOC given by the *Université de Paris-Ouest Nanterre La Défense*, entitled "*Philosophie et modes de vie (de Socrate à Pierre Hadot et Michel Foucault)*" (Philosophy and ways of life (from Socrates to Pierre Hadot and Michel Foucault)) is the second most popular (with over 10,000 enrolled students) on France's learning-management system *FUN*, after that offered by CNAM: "*Du manager au leader*" (From a manager's role to a leadership position) (over 20,000 students) which, for its part, is aimed primarily at an audience who already have a certain amount of experience in the world of business.

In fact, the audience for continuing education is divided into two unequal parts, depending on the nature of the MOOC: people who do not need to have control over the acquisition of the knowledge dispensed by the MOOC – e.g. retired people taking a MOOC for the pleasure of it, although certain septuagenarians take high-school exams; and people who need a certificate or a diploma – often for professional reasons or, in any case, to display on a CV or somewhere else.

The issue of examination was touched upon in section 3.3. If we accept the hypothesis expressed by *Coursera* that the certificates are sufficiently reliable, we begin to look for a way to distinguish and rate the different certificates awarded by MOOCs: some such certificates are sought after in the jobs market, whereas others are of interest only for the recipients. In any case, the demand for a certificate is always very high. As mentioned above, sooner or later it will be necessary to recognize the skills learned through the MOOCs if we wish to extend upon them in continuing education. Recognition of the portfolio of credentials is a crucial step. It is also possible (and indeed already happens) that certain MOOCs can award true degree certificates, with students having taken an exam in the flesh. *Coursera* is beginning to adopt this idea, offering a certificate for having completed a MOOC[12]. In order to put this idea into practice, it is necessary to hold real exams, which students must take in the flesh. This is already done by certain MOOCs: the student follows the MOOC online, but travels to a test center for the final exam. This operation can serve to generate revenue for the MOOC, because the organizer charges quite a lot of money to take the exam.

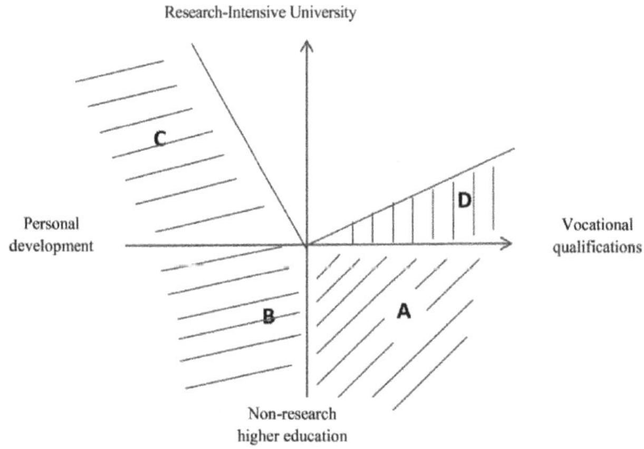

Figure 5.1. *The sphere of influence of MOOCs*

5.2.2. *Various uses for MOOCs*

People who enroll on a MOOC and actually follow it assiduously are usually pursuing a very specific objective: to gain certain specific knowledge or skills needed, for personal reasons (professional

---

12 http://chhronicle.com/blogs/wiredcampus/coursera-will-offer-certificates-for-sequences-of-moocs/.

obligations, leisure pursuits or hobbies). The figure above represents the area of MOOCs, divided between higher education with a greater or lesser research aspect, and vocational training which is more or less immediately applicable.

Sectors A and D are the areas of vocational training and lifelong learning. Sector B is the area of all possible interests, from the art of fly-fishing to the life of the Pharaohs, or the gastronomic and viticultural resources of Napa Valley, for example. Sector C is the area of people seeking to supplement, diversify or expand their existing education without necessarily needing a certification for use in the short term.

In the area of vocational qualifications, MOOCs are in competition with more-or-less prestigious qualifications and/or ones awarded by institutions considered to be average or poor. In lifelong learning, MOOCs seem to have a bright future, provided that vocational credits are validated by businesses, because they are aimed at a motivated audience whose age means that they are unable, and unwilling, to be full-time students. However, in addition to the audiences in developed countries who are over typical university age, there is an enormous potential for audiences of all ages in countries where the provision of higher education is insufficient or non-existent. Millions of young and not-so-young people are deprived of any education at all in Africa or Asia.

It is also worth mentioning the enormous potential of MOOCs within the "silver economy"[13]. The people in question are often hesitant to come regularly to classes, but are nonetheless very much involved in what is known as *therapeutic education*, which involves educating people as to how best to prevent or manage chronic illnesses. People can, and must, be taught to live more comfortably with diabetes, a variety of cancers, a neurodegenerative disease, etc. It has been proven that people who are educated about the management of their condition undergo their treatment more easily, and they can

13 This is the term used for the economy relating to people in later life (with "silver" hair).

also make use of the connective facilities of MOOCs, joining in a discussion group and feeling less isolated. The development of MOOCs such as these could be promoted by sufferers' associations. In fact, there are already educational CD-ROMs – e.g. for carers of Alzheimer's sufferers – and a MOOC would be a more interactive way of getting the relevant information across. Another prospect is the training of people caring for dependent elderly people. Family and friends, domestic support staff, carers and the staff of care homes are all potential audiences for MOOCs.

The experiments in distance learning for Africa, conducted by Albert-Claude Benhamou and his collaborators at UNF3S, demonstrate that the pursuit of a course – either available online as distance learning or distributed on a CD-ROM – is hugely important, and that people stick at it because there is no other choice. However, in order for the acquired knowledge to truly be assimilated into long-term memory, it is important for there to be local support available from tutors, throughout the whole duration of a MOOC, to answer questions, encourage people to continue with the course, put the exercises into context, and finally to award the certificate at the end of the course. It is only in these circumstances that the course is truly rewarding, and that some of the students thus taught can, in turn, act as tutors. In terms of personal development, MOOCs have a future in all domains, except for a small group of students looking for companionship-based education, with a greater or lesser level of research, with no immediate and specific objective in mind.

Apart from MOOCs for university education, we can hypothesize that MOOCs will become polarized into two main groups: MOOCs whose certificates – or, better still, degrees – are given value in the jobs market; and others which will contribute to the personal betterment of the "student" or which serve as refresher courses without an immediate simple objective.

6

Conclusions: What Does the Future Hold for MOOCs?

6.1. "To MOOC or not to MOOC"?

In the eyes of some, MOOCs are already outdated. At the very well-attended conference on online education, Online UNICA Berlin 2013, the workshop on MOOCs was introduced with the provocative title: "*MOOCs are doomed*"[1]. Among the reasons offered for this belief, Nicholas Breakwell (of Hibernia College, Ireland) argued that MOOCs represent a marketing campaign to attract students to a course; nevertheless the employment rate after graduation from a MOOC is comparable to that for a normal course, but that the MOOC costs more to implement. Another reason for skepticism is that MOOCs are not a new phenomenon.

Indeed, as indicated in Chapter 1, MOOCs represent the prolongation of the numerous experiments already performed in the areas of distance learning and *e-learning*. For those who use it, this argument is something of a double-edged sword, as it is true that distance learning has been taking place for decades and many people have successfully benefited from it. The percentage of American

1 Documents available on the conference Website: "This house believes MOOCs are doomed: the provocative motion of this year's Online EDUCA BERLIN debate". See http://www.online-educa.com/OEB_Newsportal/this-house-believes-moocs-are-doomed/.

students who have taken an online course has risen from 10% to 33% in the space of ten years, and that figure grows regularly and at a much greater rate than the number of students. In addition, the number of educators who feel that the result of online teaching is inferior to that of face-to-face teaching is decreasing constantly, and has now dropped to 25% [ALL 14].

In fact, as pointed out by Maren Deepwell (Association for Learning Technology, UK), the specific trait of MOOCs is the mass of potential learners. Hence, the challenge is to bring together "mass" and "personalization" – the same challenge faced in industrial production, where the term "*mass customization*" tends to be used; in our context, one speaks of "*personalised open education for the masses*", in accordance with the name of the project POEMs run at Strasbourg University (see section 4.1). In our view, there are two possible solutions: tutoring or intelligent *learning analytics*; in the latter case the issue becomes one of "*learning technology*". In other words, MOOCs need to be able to assess the capabilities of individual learners and adapt to play to their strengths. In the past 20 years, there has been a considerable amount of research done on the topic of distance learning systems being able to adapt to the learners. How can a system characterize a student's style and level, and in particular, identify and understand their mistakes in order to provide the appropriate correction? For an overview of the work already published in this domain, readers can refer to Eric Bruillard [BRU 97] and Monique Baron *et al.* [BAR 07]. It is likely that the wave of MOOCs will fuel further research in this area, leading to the creation of increasingly "intelligent" (or "smart") tools.

Another "counter" argument offered by some people is the failure rate – or, more accurately, the dropout rate – which sows seeds of doubt about the ability of MOOCs to adequately serve the immense need for education in the world. On this point, we can cite Rebecca Stoekle – the Vice President and Director of the Health and Technology Education Development Center, Massachusetts:

"*Certainly the MOOC in its current incarnation is already being assailed for a number of undoubted flaws: shockingly low retention rates, promulgation of an essentially isolated learning experience, few and flawed assessment measures, and especially the failure to deliver on the initial promise to offer access to high quality education to millions of youths around the world who lack access to bricks and mortar education. [...] But what if the classroom model is the wrong paradigm? What if, instead, the MOOC aimed to support a rich exchange of knowledge, skills, goods and services among a global community following the model of EBay or Patients Like Me? What if the MOOC morphed into a digital human capital value chain?*"

In many face-to-face courses, whilst the students are, in principle, present, does that necessarily mean that they are actually following the thread of the lessons? Nonetheless, around 40% of teachers questioned by the *Babson survey research group* [ALL 14] believe it is more difficult to maintain a student's interest online than in a face-to-face context. Whilst the results must be highly dependent on the type of institution and the students' age, the situation is not the same in a lecture theater of 300 students as it is in a class of 40. Certainly, though, it is true that this can present a problem if there is not tutoring system in place.

Of course, if it were possible to bring all those people who want to learn together in a lecture theater, with a teacher at the podium in front of them, there would be no need for MOOCs or for distance learning. However, when it is not possible, and given that the MOOC movement seems to be unstoppable, why should we not use this tool? Open-source software was originally met with the same skepticism. People questioned the potential quality and the motivations of the developers. Yet the opportunity for those developers to prove their talent and their know-how, in addition to the desire to demonstrate that free software can be just as good as proprietary software, has been able to put those doubts to rest, because open-source software exists today and is very widely used all over the world.

One might imagine that free MOOCs will go the same way as open-source software, and that the pleasure of putting online a worthy course, which demonstrates its developer's knowledge and didactic talent, will be a sufficient motivating force to produce a significant amount of quality content. Like it or not, MOOCs are becoming the most visible aspect of the "*Open Educational Resources*" (OER) movement, which is expanding and will, like open-source software, generate business on the side. Indeed, it is possible to imagine that a private tuition service might develop around the best MOOCs. The free courses offered by the Faculties of Medicine in many European countries have given rise to many paying services of tutoring, support, revision, preparation, etc., which are advertised around the faculty and, having conquered the preparatory year in medicine, are now expanding to influence the later years of high school.

Let us close this section of the discussion with one final criticism: some people attribute the dropout rate from MOOCs to the length of the courses and the resultant feeling of boredom. Note that this criticism is often levelled against evening classes, or any other form of teaching which comes on top of an already-hectic schedule. Sometimes, one needs real commitment to pursue an "additional" class to completion. Thus, it is worth making the courses shorter, and it was with that in mind that an entrepreneur, Pavel Dimitriev[2], came up with the idea of a "mini-MOOC", lasting just a few minutes. He set up the company *Coursmos* with the sole objective of popularizing this concept. It is teachers who place their courses online – and not necessarily for free. If a charge is made then *Coursmos* takes 9% of the profits. Another site, *Mindsky*, launched by Christian Owens and hosted by TechCrunch, also offers short courses, either individually (for $49 each) or by subscription, for $29 a month. It offers an array of 5,000 courses. In short, as we can see, the buzz caused in the area of online learning by MOOCs shows no sign of dying down. It is more than likely that numerous further initiatives will bloom in the field of MOOCs. At the very least, they have revivified and revitalized distance learning.

For our part, we have attempted to explain how MOOCs represent not a revolution but an increase in education directed at audiences who do not have easy access to education in person. Certainly, MOOCs are a form of distance learning, which, some would argue, is no substitute for being able to listen to and watch great educators

2 See http://www.journaldunet.com/management/formation/mooc-depasses.

"live". However, our view is that it is better to take a good course in MOOC format than to be deprived of an education. Furthermore, if that MOOC remains free then there can be no doubt that the movement is meritorious and should be encouraged. With this in mind, we shall now examine the ways in which to go further down the "MOOC route".

6.2. Why and for whom should MOOCs be developed?

The foregoing considerations – particularly those put forward in Chapter 5 – lead us to the conclusion that the target audience for MOOCs is not the student on the verge of entering university education. Indeed, those students, who have worked to get through their end-of-high-school exams for the sake of their parents, do not yet know who they are going to work for from hereon in, and it is often necessary to build up their motivation. Such a student can, on the other hand, freely explore the world of MOOCs and see "what is out there" to find their way. They need to be encouraged to do so by their high school, but they will go on to enroll in a university or other higher education institution. Rather than allowing high-school students free rein in front of a computer to search for post-high-school education as is currently done, it would undoubtedly be very useful to set up MOOCs which are specifically designed to guide these students through their university choices. The University of Pennsylvania offers a MOOC to foreign students to help them navigate the American university system: "Applying to US universities". This MOOC, on *Coursera*, has a paid ancillary (costing $1,100) which helps students with the filling in of the application forms, with covering letters, with the presentation of their CVs, etc. The same sort of advice is dispensed by a MOOC given by Berkeley (University of California), available on *edX*.

It is the role of higher education courses and the teachers dispensing them to aid in the construction of the personality of the young adult, helping them to find their vocation and motivation. A MOOC alone cannot fulfill that role. For that reason, the vocational MOOC will appeal mainly to fairly mature students (from graduate or master's level onwards) or to people in continuing education, who have already gained experience in the world of work and are seeking to enhance their skills or change professions, or who are looking for a job.

In addition to students, there is a broad potential target audience for MOOCs, either seeking to explore new knowledge without a particular goal (which could apply to people of any age), or seeking a financial competitive edge. In the latter case, it would tend to be people who are already certain of their vocations, looking for work, or those who have just entered the world of work, or people of any age in search of continuing education. Thus, Stanford University has put on *Coursera* a MOOC to support the establishment of startup companies: "Startup Engineering". With each person taking the MOOC having to devise their own startup project, the course includes a competition to find the best project, which stimulates healthy competitiveness. All of these audiences will require a certificate or a diploma from the MOOC.

Following our line of thought, there are at least two ways, depending on the target audience, to answer the question: why develop MOOCs?

For students who are still at university, or for those who are of student age but are unable to attend a course of study in person, we can list the following reasons for constructing MOOCs:

– to increase awareness of a topic and help those people who need to find their way in life;

– for all our students who cannot follow all the classes, often because they are obliged to work whilst they are studying;

– for all foreign students from countries with a severe deficit of higher education (e.g. countries in Africa, Asia, Latin America), provided it is possible to construct the MOOCs in the appropriate language;

– to make educational resources available to all students;

– to replace formal lectures in theaters and use MOOCs as SPOCs in a flipped-classroom context.

For universities or institutions interested by the aforelisted objectives, there is also a self-promotional aspect involved in the development of MOOCs, which can be summarized as follows:

– it helps edify and consolidate the reputation of the institution, and to "get the word out there";

– it helps attract good students from all over the world, entering master's-level study, with prestigious courses;

– it contributes to education in developing countries.

Finally, in the context of lifelong learning and personal culture, we can cite the following reasons for developing and launching MOOCs:

– specialization, improvement or expansion of professional skills, provided that the actual target of the MOOC itself is the instilment of a vocational skill;

– corporate training;

– the acquisition or sharing of expertise or wisdom, on absolutely any subject, with absolutely any recipient.

These are a number of possible objectives. We can see that they are not the same for everybody, but that they are sufficiently numerous to interest a great many people.

Holland and Trithali, in their 2014 survey [HOL 14], examine the issue from the perspective of MOOC developers, asking them what their major goals are. The respondents expressed the following goals:

– extending the reach of the institution and access to education;

– building and maintaining brand;

– improving economics by lowering costs and increasing revenues;

– improving educational outcomes for both MOOC participants and on-campus students;

– innovation in teaching and learning;

– conducting research on teaching and learning.

As regards the first listed goal, most of those interviewed mentioned continuing education, and as we have seen, this objective is certainly one of the most achievable. However, to claim, as was claimed in 2011-2012, "that quality education at mass scale and at low cost was around the corner[3]", is, as we have seen, a fallacy, because MOOCs – and flipped classrooms even more so – are expensive. Also, regardless of the scale of the course, nobody can learn without motivation. However, a MOOC on its own cannot motivate people, unless those people already have experience in the world of work.

Promoting their own image and having a brand is, as we have seen, a very common motivation for institutions.

The third listed goal, for its part, seems rather optimistic, because at present, there is no economic model which is capable of securing funding for MOOCs. The best prospect is that of lifelong learning and the obtaining and maintaining of professional skills endorsed by an industry-wide agreement on the required skills.

The fourth goal relates to improvement of the effectiveness of the teaching, and thus the educational outcome. There is now a brace of experiments which show that the use of MOOCs, flipped teaching and regular assessments, whether online or by other means, help improve students' performance – particularly for those who are not the best. This efficiency comes at a cost, and for that reason, one may well wonder whether it is possible to extend it. The second question we might as is whether it can be easily replicated. Indeed, most experiments with MOOCs, at present, are being conducted by

3 [HOL 14], p. 6. Later on, they point out (p. 7): "To date, there has been little evidence collected that would allow an assessment of whether MOOCs do indeed provide a cost-effective mechanism for producing desirable educational outcomes at scale".

highly-motivated and experienced teams of educators. Would the outcome be similar, though, if average ("lambda") teachers were in charge? It is well known that in certain domains – particularly in teaching – all experiments tend to work because of the so-called Hawthorne effect. After all, as previously stated, the human factor is absolutely crucial in education. In fact, there are no truly academic studies which have been performed on a reasonable scale. However, if "decision makers are to make rational decisions about engaging in MOOC production, it is critical to know whether MOOCs are both effective and cost-effective in delivering quality education or related outcomes[4]".

The last two objectives relate, essentially, to innovation and rejuvenation in teaching, in the vein of ideas such as flipped teaching, near-continuous assessment, the use of video and Web documents, etc. For experienced teachers, there is no doubt that the average student of today, who is familiar with the Web, with smartphones, tablets and interactive games can no longer be taught using the same "top-down" methodology as has been used for the past two millennia. Today's students have a shorter attention span, a genuine fascination with videos and visual content, and they are less capable of simply learning from a book. It is important to respond appropriately to these changed needs, and flipped teaching is certainly one possible response. Similarly, using MOOCs as a resource in a lesson is a possibility. Students today like to be active, and introduce questions; peer-assessed student presentations, even if they are often merely the culmination of various Web searches, are procedures which please the students and bring them out of the passive role they have traditionally occupied. Whilst it may be a little early and excessive to speak of a pedagogical revolution, we can see that some MOOC-supported ideas indubitably have a future.

A somewhat more distant prospect is the "mass customization" of education. In other words, is it possible, online, to tailor the course to each student on the basis of his/her reactions and results to the quizzes and other intermediary assessments? Undeniably, this is an area of research which is not a new one, but in which it is very difficult to

4 [HOL 14], p. 21.

make progress. MOOCs will bring these issues back to the forefront of the debate.

Without wishing to seem unduly optimistic, we believe that the avenues opened up by MOOCs and flipped pedagogy are worth exploring and encouraging, and for that reason, we conclude this book by asking what can be done to help facilitate the development of MOOCs. Once again, unsurprisingly, we shall see that this depends on who it is that wishes to develop a MOOC, and above all, on whom they wish to develop the course for.

6.3. What can be done to support the development of MOOCs?

6.3.1. *Hardware and software platforms*

We have already touched on the issue of the cost of MOOCs in Chapter 2. On average, we can say that a standard MOOC comprising 8 hours of classes, with the accompanying exercises, reading list and various tests, during the development and fine-tuning stages, should cost around $50,000 for 3-6 months of development work per employee. The infrastructures, the environment and the knowledge underlying the MOOC are not included in this estimation; they are supposed to be amongst the assets available to the development team, and therefore free to access. Our hypothesis is that at the institutions in question, the basic investment (development software, a studio, etc.) is made as a one-off, and does not come out of the development team's budget. The same is not true of the human resources involved in the work, and therein lies the marginal cost of the MOOC. In higher education institutions, if we wish to encourage the development of MOOCs, we need to regard this development work as being part of the teachers' normal duties. The cost for the institution is the cost involved in replacing the teacher to impart classes which he/she used to teach face-to-face. Yet it is still difficult to draw a conclusive balance because, if the MOOC is effectively used, it will bring savings in terms of teachers' time because the same course can be used several times over. In any case, the time spent on the design and construction of a MOOC by teachers should be taken into account as part of their normal workload, and paid as such. Note that at present, this recognition is not necessarily a given; often it is the person in question, who is passionate about new technologies, who makes the investment *gratis pro deo*. If universities want their teachers to engage in the construction of MOOCs, the universities need to seriously consider giving incentives to those teachers; the first urgent point is that the construction of a MOOC must be considered to be not a hobby but a teaching duty like any other. However, the universities also need to be aware of the fact that the activity does not produce immediate gains, except in terms of image and attraction of new groups of students. It is their responsibility, depending on the context, to set aside a portion of their budgets for these projects, and/or find resources from other sources (e.g. donations, calls for tender on a national and international scale, etc.).

The second idea as to how to help relates to the material resources needed to construct a MOOC – particularly the technological resources. To build a MOOC in reasonable conditions, and with a sufficient level of quality (with which, as we have seen, there can be no compromise), it is necessary to have a "studio", or at least have equipment to film the class, create a montage with the footage, and inject animation into the lecture whilst recording. Also, though, we need "editing" software (which is as necessary for MOOCs as is page-setting software for book production). Finally, we need a server – a high-powered server if we are anticipating a large number of connections – which we are able to operate and maintain. Together, the "editor" software and the "server" hardware, along with service software (for answering questions, setting up forums, managing enrollments, relations with the teachers, statistics, etc.), constitutes a *MOOC platform*. Yet readers must bear in mind that whilst the editor and the service software represent a certain amount of effort in terms of development, they are not enormous, and therefore the investment made for these modules is not extraordinary – especially since there are open-source software packages available and that existing learning-management systems such as *Moodle* can be adapted to the task. On the other hand, having a server, or better, a *Cloud*, capable of handling 50,000 connections without being overloaded, represents a not-insignificant cost, as do competent operating engineers. Although we often use the umbrella term "MOOC platform", which covers both the software and hardware, we must not lose sight of the fact that they are separate entities, and that it is perfectly possible for two systems to use the same software but have separate servers. The associated costs are not the same either.

Who should supply the "MOOC factories" and portals? As we have just seen, the universities are encouraged to do so for reasons of brand and standing. For the universities, as we have also seen, the objective would be to equip or enhance the skills of a pre-existing multimedia or distance-learning department. Thus, Armando Fox has recently been appointed Faculty Director of Berkeley's MOOCLab, which extends Berkeley existing online education programs; we see the same situation in many other US universities as well.

The response is different for many other actors who do not have experience of online education, and who may be tempted to construct MOOCs for a wide variety of reasons: tourism, proper use of resources made available to the public (e.g. in the area of healthcare), children's activities for primary and secondary schools, continuing education for local-government agents and employees of businesses, etc. These various actors will find there is a rich market offering platforms and services to develop and host their MOOCs. A major city could quite easily post its MOOCs aimed at primary and secondary schools on one platform, and those devoted to tourism on another. Having a Website or access to a MOOC portal seems, to us, a realistic objective for many institutions, in both the public and private sectors. It is very likely that, in the coming years, we shall see the emergence of several models of platforms and server-clustering, but what is essential is to have a visible gateway offering all sorts of courses to a geographically-limited and demanding audience. Once that gateway is up and running, the next step is to incentivize the construction of MOOCs.

6.3.2. *Encouragement of developers*

One could be forgiven for thinking, first of all, that those who have an interest in developing MOOCs, for the reasons discussed in section

6.2, would do so without any other incentive, and that therefore there is no need to interfere. This is probably what would happen in universities and schools if they were given the appropriate resources. When a MOOC is being developed for reasons of prestige, the wheels have already been set in motion, and the project will carry itself forward under its own momentum. If the MOOC is for internal use, to launch a sort of flipped-teaching policy or for use as a SPOC, there will surely need to be an overarching policy and incentives offered by the establishment, even if only, as discussed above, in terms of acknowledging and remunerating the investments made by the teachers themselves.

For large territorial communities, there is an immediate advantage to encouraging the development of MOOCs relating to the municipality's resources, museums, history, restaurants, gastronomy, etc. Hence, the celebrated chef Alain Ducasse needed no incentives from the state to launch his virtual campus, offering courses in cookery and gastronomy, inspired by the model of the *Khan Academy*. All these courses, designed mainly for tourists, or simply for people curious about history and customs different to their own, fit in very well with the philosophy of MOOCs. Versions of the courses offered in the various languages spoken by tourists to the area would certainly be a welcome development. Yet the development and distribution of these courses is more significant than it might seem, because a dedicated MOOC platform would be a new concept, and would offer local creative talent an outlet. MOOCs could be constructed at a "*MOOC house*" where the designers would have access to information, expertise and support, a studio and a platform for the operation of the course (excluding premises costs and operating expenditure, the investment required would be around $500,000, but the costs of software and hardware could be shared between a number of institutions). At the very least, it seems important for each major collective to follow Boston's example and have a MOOC portal, with or without a partner, so as to have a single space in which to exhibit the online creativity of all those wishing to "instruct and educate" the public both in the region and beyond.

6.4. What can be done to support the users of MOOCs?

In order to get the most out of a MOOC, of course a potential student needs a computer, but also it is preferable that he/she not be completely isolated. The testimony of many people attests to the need of people assiduously following a MOOC to be able to come together and exchange ideas. This is the movement of *meetups* (see section 3.4). Of course, learners have the means to communicate with one another online (forums, chatrooms, etc.), but conducting exchanges in person is something quite different. At the Online EDUCA Berlin conference in December 2013, a participant from Frankfurt who had already successfully completed several MOOCs explained how he had set up a group of 72 MOOCers from the city who met up regularly in person. On this point, two strategies can be envisaged: either we support the construction of a network and/or forum which enables MOOC users to help and encourage one another, or we provide "tutors". In terms of the first suggestion, the simplest thing to do is provide MOOCers with meeting places in local communities, where they can find all information regarding MOOCs, and possibly kiosks to follow the courses if they do not have a computer of their own.

In countries where the provision of higher education or vocational training is insufficient or non-existent, the use of MOOCs is not a Utopian prospect; in actual fact, it is an urgent need which both governments and charities ought to encourage and even fund. As we have seen, in order for this strategy to work, it is important to have one or more tutors based locally, who can encourage the participants to keep pace with the rhythm of the course, comment on and correct the exercises, and even add some exercises of their own. Tutors are very useful in helping to detect the most frequent mistakes or misunderstandings, and also serve as an interface with the team in charge of the MOOC.

As noted above, this way of working has been shown by experience to be extremely productive. In addition, it opens up the possibility of having the tutor administer an exam locally. To our minds, this is, by far, the best way of working with distant institutions in countries or regions where higher education is not yet firmly rooted, or indeed is non-existent. It is essential, of course, for the tutors to have received prior instruction and maintain a link with the MOOC team. Tutor training could be one way of helping both the designers and the users of MOOCs. The training of tutors in countries where the provision of higher education is famously inadequate would be one way to help certain developing countries. It is envisageable that tutors could be educated at universities to support one or more MOOCs designed by those universities, like nurse training.

6.5. A step towards digital learning houses (DLHs)

If we take a step back and gain a little perspective, we can see that MOOCs in higher education are likely to develop gradually, for pedagogical reasons (SPOCs) or reasons of prestige. Under pressure from their competitors, certain institutions will not hesitate to use MOOCs, and flipped teaching, as a sales point. Hence, as requested by students, classes in lecture theaters will gradually be phased out in the early years of university. There is certainly no need to intervene in this evolution which, like all "digital revolutions", will take place rather slowly but inescapably.

However, lifelong education is an area in which a voluntaristic policy would be welcome. We have seen that MOOCs can be addressed to very broad and varied audiences. Lifelong learning is, at present, desperately lacking in many countries, as is training for the careers of the future. Schools are unable to adapt fast enough, when they are clearly behind in terms of job opportunities; the same is often true of the many educational organizations which are oriented more by the needs of the trainers than those of the students/interns. Because of the very rapid economic and social changes occurring in today's world, schools are faced with the difficulty of having to prepare students for jobs which do not even exist yet, the nature of which no-one is able to predict with certainty. Hence, there is a never-ending problem of adapting the existing educational offering to nascent jobs. MOOCs can certainly provide flexibility and offer quicker responses than a traditional school. We are already witnessing this phenomenon in the area of computer science.

Creating spaces where job-seekers and those seeking to evolve can find information online about the education on offer, the right to education and the best MOOCs to prepare for their chosen career paths would certainly be a great help to the population. These sorts of new-generation "*learning centers*", promoting MOOCs, are probably one of the possible futures for libraries when, in less than fifteen years, all books are digitized and it is possible to obtain an individual paper copy with POD (*Print on Demand*). The City of Boston, in collaboration with *edX*, undertook an experiment of this type known as *BostonX*. The aim was to make MOOCs available to Boston citizens at their local libraries, and to "*community college*" students[5] at their college.

Whether in "new age" libraries or *ad hoc* centers, *digital learning houses (DLHs)* will, in addition to information, offer a studio for the creation of MOOCs, competent personnel to give guidance on the appropriate software, the services of small companies specializing in MOOC construction, and all of this will help the designers of MOOCs. DLHs would also have a "showroom" and an event venue for MOOC startup companies.

These centers could also be equipped with computer kiosks to enable those who do not have a computer or a conducive environment at home to work with MOOCs on site. These people could also have hours of computer use to look for or apply for jobs online.

Finally, these centers could have meeting rooms for those pursuing a given MOOC who wish to meet up and talk in person, meet with tutors or other people who have already completed the MOOC, or who have a good knowledge of the subject in question. They would be forums for intergenerational exchanges for MOOCers wishing to meet up: especially those on cMOOCS.

5 https:/www.bostonmagazine.com/news/article/2013/04/02/boston-online-education/.

Bibliography

[ALL 14] ALLEN I.E., SEAMAN J., *Grade Change, tracking Online Education in the United States*, Babson Survey Research Group, Pearson and Sloan-C, 2014.

[BAR 07] BARON M., GUIN D., TROUCHE L. (eds.), *Environnements informatisés et ressources numériques pour l'apprentissage: conception et usages, regards croisés*, Editions Hermès-Lavoisier, Paris, 2007.

[BRI 13] BRIAND M., "Autour des MOOC", a collection of articles. Available at http://www.intercoop.info/index.php?title=Autour_des_MOOC, 2013.

[BRU 97] BRUILLARD É., *Les machines à enseigner*, Éditions Hermès, Paris, 1997.

[CHR 13] CHRISTIENSEN G., STEINMETZ A., ALCORN B., *et al.*, "The MOOC phenomenon: who takes massive open online courses and why", Working paper, University of Pennsylvania, 2013. Available at http://papers.ssrn.com/sol3/papers.cfm?abstract id=2350964.

[CHO 14] CHOUK I., FLEURY J.B., "La résistance aux MOOC: le cas des SPOC", Forthcoming, University of Cergy-Pontoise, 2014.

[COR 10] CORMIER D., SIEMENS G., "Through the open door: open courses as research, learning and engagement", *EDUCAUSE Review*, vol. 54, no. 4, pp. 30–39, 2010. Available at http://www.educause.edu/ero/article/through-the-open-door-open-courses-research-learning-and-engagement.

[DAT 12] DATIN V., "MOOC francophone", Available at http://www.scoop.it/moocfrancophone, 2012

[EPE 12] EPELBOIN Y., "MOOC: a European view", December 2012. Available at http://wiki.upmc.fr/x/RICP.

[GAE 13] GAEBEL M., "MOOCs Massive Online Courses", EUA Occasional Papers, January 2013. Available at http://www.eua.be.

[FOX 13] FOX A., "From MOOCs to SPOCs", *Communications of the ACM*, vol. 56, no. 12, pp. 38–40, 2013.

[GIL 13] GILLIOT J.-M., BARTHOLET J., "Universités en ligne, une révolution dans le monde de l'enseignement", *Pour la Science*, no. 431, pp. 33–49, September 2013.

[GIL 13] GILLOIS P., PAGONIS D., VUILLEZ J.P., *et al.*, Réforme pédagogique et "e-learning" pour le concours de première année à la faculté de médecine de Grenoble: satisfaction des étudiants et des enseignants, *La presse médicale*, vol. 42, no. 2, pp. 44–52, 2013.

[HAR 12] HARDEN N., "The End of the University as We Know it", *The American Interest*, vol. 8, no. 3, December 2012.

[HOL 14] HOLLANDS F., TRITHALI D., "MOOCs: Expectations and Reality. Full Report", Center for Benefit-Cost Studies of Education, Teachers College, Columbia University, NY, 2014. Available at http://www.academicpartnerships.com/sites/default/files/MOOCs_Expectations_and_Reality.pdf.

[KAR 13] KARSENTI T., "Les MOOC, révolution ou simple effet de mode?", *Revue Internationale des Technologies en pédagogie universitaire*, vol. 10, no. 2, pp. 6–21, 2013.

[KAS 14] KASSABIAN D.W., "The value of MOOCs to early adopter universities", *Educause Review on line*, vol. 16, June 2014. Available at http://www.educause.edu/ero/article/value-moocs-early-adopter-universities.

[KHA 12] KHAN S., *The One World Schoolhouse: Education Reimagined*, Grand Central Publishing, New York, 2012.

[KOH 13] KOHLER F., JAY N., DUCREAU F., *et al.*, "Courlis (Cours en ligne de statistiques appliquées). Un MOOC francophone innovant", *Hegel*, vol. 3, no. 1, 2013.

[KOL 13] KOLLER D., NG A., DO C., *et al.*, "Retention and intention in massive open online courses: in depth", *Educause Review on line*, June 2013. Available at http://www.educause.edu/ero/article/retention-and-intention-massive-open-online-courses-depth.

[LER 12] LEARNING ANALYTICS, Policy Brief, UNESCO Institute for Information Technology in Education, November 2012. Available at http://iite.unesco.org/policy_briefs/.

[LER 14] LERU ADVICE PAPER, Online learning at research intensive universities, no. 16, 2014. Available at www.leru.org/index.php/public/extra/advice-papers/.

[LIY 12] LIYANAGUNAWARDENA T.R., ADAMS A.A., WILLIAMS S.A., *MOOCs: A Systematic Study of the Published Literature*, 2008–2012. Available at http://www.irrodl.org/index.php/irrodl/article/view/1455/2531.

[MAC 88] MACCOBY M., *Why Work*, Simon and Schuster, NY, 1988.

[MAS 14] MASSIVE OPEN ONLINE COURSE, Wikipedia, http://en.wikipedia.org/wiki/MOOC.

[MOO 14] MOOC NEWSLETTER, daily publication. Available at http://www.mooc.ca/.

[NOR 14] NORWEGIAN REPORT, NOU 2014:5 MOOCs for Norway. Available at http://www.regjeringen.no/pages/38804804/PDFS/NOU201420140005000EN_PDFS.pdf.

[OPE 14] OPEN EDUCATION EUROPA. Available at: http://www.Open education europa.eu.

[QUE 13] QUENTIN I., "Revue de la littérature nord-américaine sur les apprenants de MOOCs" (in French), November 2013. Available at http://isabellequentin.wordpress.com/2013/11/03/revue-de-la-litterature-Snord-americaine-sur-les-apprenants-de-moocs/.

[SHA 13] SHARPLES M., MCANDREW P., WELLER M., *et al.*, Innovating Pedagogy 2013, Report 2 from Open University, The Open University, September 2013, http://www.open.ac.uk/blogs/innovating/.

[THE XX] THE MOOC GUIDE. Available at https://sites.google.com/site/themoocguide/.

[VAR 12] VARDI M.Y., "Will MOOCs Destroy Academia", *Communications of the ACM*, vol. 55, no. 11, p. 5, 2012.

[WAT 91] WATKINS B.L., "A quite radical idea: the invention and elaboration of collegiate correspondence study", in WATKINS B.L., WRIGHT S.J. (eds.), *The Foundation of American Distance Education: A Century of Collegiate Correspondence Study*, Kendall/Hunt Pub., Dubuque IO, pp. 1–35, 1991.

[YUA 14] YUAN L., POWELL S., OLIVIER B., *Beyond MOOCs: Sustainable Online Learning in Institutions*, CETIS publications, January 2014. Available at http://publications.cetis.ac.uk/2014/898.

Glossary of Terms

ACE	American Council of Education
ALISON	Advanced Learning Interactive Systems Online
AUF	*Agence Universitaire de la Francophonie*
AWS	Advanced Web Service
CBS	Columbia Broadcasting System
CNAM	*Conservatoire National des Arts et Métiers*
DLH	Digital Learning House
DWE	Digital Work Environment
EADTU	European Association of Distance Teaching Universities
ECTS	European Credits Transfer System
EDHEC	*Ecole des Hautes Etudes Commerciales*
ENS	*Ecole Normale Supérieure (Paris)*
EPFL	*Ecole Polytechnique Fédérale de Lausanne*

FERPA	Family Educational Rights and Privacy Act
FICC	Face-to-Face Interactive Complementary Class
FUN	*France Université Numérique*
HTML	HyperText Mark-Up Language
IaaS	Infrastructure as a Service
LERU	League of European Research Universities
LMS	Learning Management System
MCQs	Multiple-Choice Questions
MOOCs	Massive online open courses
NIH	Not invented here
NYU	New-York University
ODE	Open Distance Education
OER	Open Educational Resources
OLI	Open Learning Initiative
OU	Open University (UK)
OUC	Open University of China
PBS	Public Broadcasting Service
PDF	Portable Document Format
POD	Print on Demand
POEMs	Personalised Open Education for the Masses
SaaS	Software as a service
SAIL	Structured, Active, In-class Learning Program (U-Penn)
SEE	Stanford Engineering Everywhere

SOOC	Small Open Online Courses
SMS	Short Message Service
SPIRAL	*Serveur Pédagogique Interactif de Ressources d'Apprentissage de Lyon 1*
SPOC	Small Private Online Classes
TA	Teaching Assistant
TIL	*Trans Innov Longévité (distance course awarding a master's degree in gerontology)*
TORC	Tiny Online Restricted Course
UD	University Degree (a qualification awarded by a university which is not national; it is generally associated with continuing education, and is not free)
UNF3S	*Université Numérique des Sciences de la Santé et du Sport*
UNISCIEL	*Université Numérique des Sciences en Ligne*
UPMC	*Université Pierre et Marie Curie, Paris*
VLE	Virtual Learning Environment
WGU	Western Governors University

Index

E, F, G

H, I

J, K, L

M

N, O, P

U, V, X, Y

Other titles from

ISTE

in

Information Systems, Web and Pervasive Computing

2014

DINET Jérôme
Information Retrieval in Digital Environments

KEMBELLEC Gérald, CHARTRON Ghislaine, SALEH Imad
Recommender Systems

VENTRE Daniel
Chinese Cybersecurity and Defense

2013

BERNIK Igor
Cybercrime and Cyberwarfare

CAPET Philippe, DELAVALLADE Thomas
Information Evaluation

LEBRATY Jean-Fabrice, LOBRE-LEBRATY Katia
Crowdsourcing: One Step Beyond

2012

GAUSSIER Eric, YVON François
Textual Information Access

STOCKINGER Peter
Audiovisual Archives: Digital Text and Discourse Analysis

VENTRE Daniel
Cyber Conflict

2011

LEMBERGER Pirmin, MOREL Mederic
managing Complexity of Information Systems

STOCKINGER Peter
Introduction to Audiovisual Archives

STOCKINGER Peter
Digital Audiovisual Archives

VENTRE Daniel
Cyberwar and Information Warfare

2010

BONNET Pierre
Enterprise Data Governance

2009

BONNET Pierre, DETAVERNIER Jean-Michel, VAUQUIER Dominique
Sustainable IT Architecture: the Progressive Way of Overhauling Information Systems with SOA

PAPY Fabrice
Information Science

RIVARD François, ABOU HARB Georges, MERET Philippe
The Transverse Information System

VENTRE Daniel
Information Warfare

2008

MANOUVRIER Bernard, LAURENT Ménard
Application Integration: EAI, B2B, BPM and SOA

PAPY Fabrice
Digital Libraries

2006

CORNIOU Jean-Pierre
Looking Back and Going Forward in IT

Printed and Bound by CPI Group (UK) Ltd, Croydon, CR0 4YY

d and bound by CPI Group (UK) Ltd, Croydon, CR0 4YY
13/09/2026
14961018-0002